Romans

INTERPRETATION
BIBLE STUDIES

Other Interpretation Bible Studies
from Westminster John Knox Press

Romans

ART ROSS AND MARTHA STEVENSON

WESTMINSTER
JOHN KNOX PRESS
LOUISVILLE · KENTUCKY

Scripture quotations, unless otherwise noted, are from New Revised Standard Version of the Bible, copyright © 1989 by Division of Christian Education of the National Council of the Churches of Christ in America.

The photographs on pages 1, 5, 10, 15, 21, 22, 32, 34, 36, 45, 52, 56, 58, 65, 69, and 73 are © 1998 PhotoDisc, Inc. All rights reserved. Used by permission.

Book design by Drew Stevens
Cover design by Pam Poll
Cover illustration by Robert Stratton

First Edition
Published by Westminster John Knox Press
Louisville, Kentucky

This book is printed on acid-free paper that meets the American National Standards Institute Z39.48 standard. ♾

PRINTED IN THE UNITED STATES OF AMERICA

05 06 07 08 — 10 9 8 7 6 5 4

Library of Congress Cataloging-in-Publication Data

A catalog record for this book is available from the Library of Congress.

ISBN 0-664-22646-9

Contents

Series Introduction

The Bible has long been revered for its witness to God's presence and redeeming activity in the world; its message of creation and judgment, love and forgiveness, grace and hope; its memorable characters and stories; its challenges to human life; and its power to shape faith. For generations people have found in the Bible inspiration and instruction, and, for nearly as long, commentators and scholars have assisted students of the Bible. This series, Interpretation Bible Studies (IBS), continues that great heritage of scholarship with a fresh approach to biblical study.

Designed for ease and flexibility of use for either personal or group study, IBS helps readers not only to learn about the history and theology of the Bible, understand the sometimes difficult language of biblical passages, and marvel at the biblical accounts of God's activity in human life, but also to accept the challenge of the Bible's call to discipleship. IBS offers sound guidance for deepening one's knowledge of the Bible and for faithful Christian living in today's world.

IBS was developed out of three primary convictions. First, the Bible is the church's scripture and stands in a unique place of authority in Christian understanding. Second, good scholarship helps readers understand the truths of the Bible and sharpens their perception of God speaking through the Bible. Third, deep knowledge of the Bible bears fruit in one's ethical and spiritual life.

Each IBS volume has ten brief units of key passages from a book of the Bible. By moving through these units, readers capture the sweep of the whole biblical book. Each unit includes study helps, such as maps, photos, definitions of key terms, questions for reflection, and suggestions for resources for further study. In the back of each volume is a Leader's Guide that offers helpful suggestions on how to use IBS.

The Interpretation Bible Studies series grows out of the well-known Interpretation commentaries (John Knox Press), a series that helps preachers and teachers in their preparation. Although each IBS volume bears a deep kinship to its companion Interpretation commentary, IBS can stand alone. The reader need not be familiar with the Interpretation commentary to benefit from IBS. However, those who want to discover even more about the Bible will benefit by consulting Interpretation commentaries too.

Through the kind of encounter with the Bible encouraged by the Interpretation Bible Studies, the church will continue to discover God speaking afresh in the scriptures.

Introduction to Romans

This book began as a church Bible study of Paul's letter to the Christian community in Rome. For nine weeks, about one hundred members of White Memorial Presbyterian Church in Raleigh, North Carolina, came together for an hour and a half on Monday nights. Educated, committed adults listened, questioned, and pondered Paul's words. Class members did not find the study easy, but most remained committed to the process. Many found Romans rewarding, even exciting. This book reflects their questions and insights.

The authors of this book are a pastor who enjoys teaching and a church educator who values challenging students of the Bible to think about our shared faith. Our desire, both in the class and in this book, is to explore Romans and to learn how Romans has made important contributions to the Christian church.

The letter to the Romans is a tough book to read and to study. Parts of the book soar; other parts drag. At times Paul reveals insights into the nature of God and the power of the gospel that make the reader shout, "Hallelujah!" On other occasions, the most diligent student will wonder exactly what Paul means or even will ask, "How did this book get into the Bible?" Whatever our response to Romans may be, the affirmation of the church across the years is that the letter to the Romans is essential to Christian life and faith.

Romans contains some of the most beloved passages in the New Testament. Words from Romans 8 are often read at funerals, and portions of Romans 7 eloquently describe the human predicament of sin. Many Christians have memorized portions of chapter 12, with the magnificent call, "Do not be conformed to this world, but be transformed by the renewing of your minds, so that you may discern what is the will of God." Other parts of the letter, such as Paul's efforts to reconcile God's covenant promise to Israel with the Christian affirmation of the Lordship of Christ and the new covenant, are invaluable even though complex.

Paul's letter to the Romans is the first of the Pauline epistles to appear in the New Testament; it is also the longest and the most theologically significant. Romans had great influence on Martin Luther, opening the way to the Protestant Reformation. John Calvin was devoted to the study of Romans, and the letter became a major influence in Calvin's understanding of theology and church government. John Wesley, upon hearing Luther's Preface to Romans, declared that he felt his heart "strangely warmed." In our own century, Karl Barth's commentary *The Epistle to the Romans* has exerted great power in reshaping Christian preaching and thinking.

Romans is not history or narrative. It is not even a "letter" in the usual sense of that word. Romans is early Christian education; as Anselm said of theology in the eleventh century, it is "faith seeking understanding." Romans is Paul's desire, led by the Holy Spirit, to explain and to affirm what has happened in human lives and in the whole of creation, through the life, death, and resurrection of Christ and through the establishment of the church.

Reading Romans may remind some of a class in solid geometry or organic chemistry, or of the struggle many have in learning to operate a computer. The language and ideas at first appear impossible to grasp, but then a breakthrough

---

Righteousness through Faith

21 But now, apart from <u>law</u>, the <u>righteousness</u> of God has been disclosed, and is attested by the law and the prophets, 22 the righteousness of God through faith in Jesus Christ for all who believe. For there is no distinction, 23 since all have sinned and fall short of the glory of God; 24 they are now <u>justified</u> by his <u>grace</u> as a gift, through the <u>redemption</u> that is in Christ Jesus, 25 whom God put forward as a <u>sacrifice</u> of <u>atonement</u>[l] by his <u>blood</u>, effective through <u>faith</u>. He did this to show his righteousness, because in his <u>divine forbearance</u> he had passed over the sins previously committed; 26 it was to prove at the present time that he himself is righteous and that he justifies the one who has faith in Jesus.[m]

occurs, and the message begins to take on great meaning. We can ignore Romans and stick to the Gospels or to other Pauline letters, just as we could skip geometry or chemistry in school or never learn to use a computer. Our "salvation" does not depend on understanding Romans. However, the study of difficult subjects, even if we never master them, expands and enhances all of life; so, too, does grappling with Romans expand and enhance our Christian faith.

Romans, by Paul J. Achtemeier, in the series Interpretation: A Bible Commentary for Teaching and Preaching, was a companion guide, along with the Bible (NRSV). Frequent references are made to Achtemeier's excellent commentary. Additional resources are listed in the Bibliography. As we worked through Romans, we repeatedly realized that Paul uses certain words in a unique way. Words that need to be pondered in the context of Paul's larger message are set in italic type.

> ## Want to Know More?
>
> **About leading Bible study groups?** See Roberta Hestenes, *Using the Bible in Groups* (Philadelphia: Westminster Press, 1983).
>
> **About studying Romans?** See Paul J. Achtemeier, *Romans,* Interpretation (Atlanta: John Knox Press, 1985); David L. Bartlett, *Romans,* Westminster Bible Companion (Louisville, Ky.: Westminster John Knox Press, 1995); and William Barclay, *The Letter to the Romans,* Daily Study Bible (Philadelphia: Westminster Press, 1975).
>
> **About Paul's writings?** See Calvin J. Roetzel, *The Letters of Paul: Conversations in Context,* 4th ed. (Louisville, Ky.: Westminster John Knox Press, 1998).

The importance of Romans and the uniqueness of vocabulary is emphasized in these comments from Martin Luther at the close of the Introduction to his *Commentary on Romans:*

> In this Epistle we find most richly the things that a Christian ought to know: namely, what is law, Gospel, sin, punishment, grace, faith, righteousness, Christ, God, good works, love, hope, the cross, and also how we are to conduct ourselves toward everyone, whether righteous or sinner, strong or weak, friend or foe. All this is ably founded on Scripture and proved by his [Paul's] own example and that of the prophets. Therefore it appears that St. Paul wanted to comprise briefly in this one Epistle the whole Christian and evangelical doctrine and to prepare an introduction to the entire Old Testament; for, without doubt, he who has this epistle well in his heart, has the light and power of the Old Testament with him. Therefore let every Christian exercise himself in it habitually and continually. To this may God give His grace. Amen. (Luther, xxvi)

1   Background to Romans

Linked to the Old Testament —Source of Life for the Church

Before reading an actual biblical text, serious students will find help in reflecting on the context within which the text was first written and first read. In the best tradition of the Christian faith, tested wisdom says that studying a biblical text without paying attention to the historical and theological context of the passage can reduce the Bible to a pretext for our own insights and beliefs.

"Study of the epistles isolated from their context is like reading the answers at the end of an algebra book without the corresponding problems." Calvin J. Roetzel, *The Letters of Paul: Conversations in Context,* 4th ed. (Louisville, Ky.: Westminster John Knox Press, 1998), 79.

Paul wrote his letter to a specific congregation, living in a particular place, at a certain time. But the letter has important links to the larger world and to distant times. The author was an "Old Testament person." Paul had grown up in the synagogue. He knew the literature of Judaism. His faith was shaped by the stories of Adam and Eve, Abraham and Sarah, Jacob, Joseph, Moses, and Miriam. These stories gave specific content to Paul's understanding of God and to his understanding of human history. Throughout Romans, Paul makes frequent reference to Old Testament people and events, especially those found in the opening chapters of Genesis.

Grounded in the Old Testament

As preparation for reading and studying Romans, think about the events that contribute to the Old Testament. Remember Adam and Eve in the Garden of Eden, the encounter with the serpent, the desire to "be like God, knowing good and evil" (Gen. 3:5). In Romans, Paul interprets these events and gives great significance to "Adam's sin."

To capture the biblical and theological context within which Romans was written, recall the story of the tower of Babel. That ancient passage tells how the human ability to master technology resulted in idolatry: "Come, let us build ourselves a city, and a tower with its top in the heavens, and let us make a name for ourselves; otherwise we shall be scattered abroad upon the face of the whole earth" (Gen. 11:4). Paul knows the deceptive power of the human desire to make our life secure.

After Genesis reveals the power of pride and rebellion to create alienation both among human beings and between human beings and God, attention turns toward covenant. God calls Abraham and Sarah, saying, "Go from your country and your kindred and your father's house to the land that I will show you. I will make of you a great nation, and I will bless you, and make your name great, so that you will be a blessing" (Gen. 12:1–2). This promise makes God "righteous," says Paul, and the gospel proclaims that the righteousness of God is fully revealed in the life, death, and resurrection of Jesus. In the Old Testament, circumcision becomes a sign of this promise.

The Abraham and Sarah story leads to the saga of Esau and Jacob, in which Jacob cheats his brother Esau out of his birthright. Jacob's uncle Laban then cheats Jacob out of his rightful wife. Jacob's sons sell their own brother, Joseph, into slavery. Joseph becomes a person of power and wisdom who ultimately rescues his entire family from famine. However, the rescue brings the family

Paul draws upon the scriptures to speak to the Romans.

to Egypt where, after years go by, they become slaves. God sends Moses to rescue the Hebrews and leads them to the land first promised to Abraham and Sarah. The journey to the Promised Land includes the giving of the Ten Commandments at Mount Sinai. The commandments become the law, which is the foundation of the Jewish faith and which shapes Paul's earliest identity.

Life in the wilderness prepares the Hebrew people for the battles of conquest that lead to the establishment of the nation Israel.

Government by judges and prophets gives way to the rule of kings. The rule of kings leads to corruption and division of the nation into the ten northern tribes of Israel and the two southern tribes of Judah. Military conquest occurs. Israel is destroyed, and Judah is taken into exile. The temple, a symbol of both covenant and law, is destroyed, and the sacred city of Jerusalem is reduced to rubble. In the wilderness of exile, the prophets give voice to a "messianic hope," the expectation that God will come to redeem God's people. God will come, not as a mighty warrior after the manner of King David, but as a suffering servant.

In time, the exiles are allowed to return to Jerusalem, and the temple is eventually rebuilt. Rabbinic Judaism, based upon strict observance of the law, begins to emerge. The messianic hope remains. Roman occupation occurs.

Paul, a Product of His Times

Into this history, Paul, first known as Saul, is born. He is a "member of the people of Israel, of the tribe of Benjamin, a Hebrew born of Hebrews; . . . a Pharisee" (Phil. 3:5). His world was shaped by the events of the Old Testament; his faith in God was the faith of Abraham and Sarah, of Moses and Miriam, of King David, and of Isaiah and Jeremiah. Paul treasured the Law of God, the worship in the temple, and the life of faith as he knew it.

Then, to Paul's amazement, God appeared to him, Christ spoke to him, and his world was changed forever. Paul began to see in Jesus—and in the church which came into being through the story of Jesus' life, death, and resurrection—the proof of God's power to fulfill the promise first made to Abraham and Sarah. Paul writes Romans from the viewpoint of a person whose life has been transformed, not by personal encounter with Jesus but by the power of God revealed through Jesus by the Holy Spirit.

Paul not only knew the Jewish way of life, he also understood something of the Greek culture and the Roman culture. Rome ruled the world of Paul's day. Latin was the "imperial" language. Greece was the source of wisdom and philosophy. Scholarly debate drew upon the writings of Plato and Socrates. Hebrew was the language of

"The letter is full of Paul's passion for the gospel of Jesus Christ. For him, and he believes for all humankind, Jesus is the one in whom God turns human history around, doing what is right for the Roman Christians and for the whole creation."—David L. Bartlett, *Romans,* Westminster Bible Companion, 3.

the law; Greek was the language in which the New Testament, including Romans, was written. Latin was the language of Rome. Paul's letter, like his life and his faith, embraces and transcends three great cultural traditions of the day.

Thinking the Way Paul Thought

The human mind uses ideas and concepts to shape the way we process information. Ideas and concepts then take the form of words. Words, especially words that speak of faith, are symbols for complex thoughts and ideas. Twenty years ago, the request "Please type a letter" would mean, "Please go to a typewriter and sit down behind it; type out the words I will dictate to you. If you make a mistake, you will need to type the letter again. If multiple copies are needed, carbon paper will be used." Today those same words mean something very different. The request "Please type me a letter" is code for saying, "Please use a computer and a word processing system to generate a letter I will give you. If you make a mistake, the computer will catch it and correct it. If you need multiple copies, either a printer or a copier will provide them easily and quickly, or else the letter will simply be distributed by electronic mail, never using paper." A letter is still a letter, but the ways we think about producing and delivering a letter have dramatically changed, though the language remains the same.

> "*Romans*, of all Paul's letters, comes nearest to being a theological treatise."—William Barclay, *The Letter to the Romans*, Daily Study Bible, 1.

For Paul, the gospel and the Holy Spirit change the ways we think about God and the ways we think about ourselves and other people as dramatically as the computer changes the way we think about producing a letter.

An essential part of hearing Paul's message to the Romans, which is also the message of God to the church in every time and place, is learning the meaning of the words, ideas, and concepts that Paul uses. A study of Romans requires us to learn a new vocabulary, just as we might do when learning to operate a computer. Paul uses words and ideas we know, but he uses the words and ideas in new ways that sometimes confuse us.

> "Paul deals with problems as contemporary as tomorrow's newspapers."—Paul J. Achtemeier, *Romans*, Interpretation, 1.

For Paul, faith words take on meaning within human history. History is the context within which faith language has meaning. A major way of thinking about reality is to distinguish between "history" and "knowledge." Both history and knowledge can be seen as the arena for divine activity. History is the realm of the concrete; specific events occur in the world, and these events determine the course of other events. Knowledge is more abstract; it is the world of ideas and beliefs, as opposed to that of actions. The Christian affirmation is that, in Jesus, God entered human history. Because of Jesus, Christians are convinced that the course of history is forever changed. For Paul, the establishment of the church among the Gentiles is a dramatic confirmation of the power of God and of the power of the gospel to bring creation to fulfillment. What God has done and will do in history, not what we "know" or "believe" about God, becomes the foundation of our faith and defines reality.

> "Only when [God] brings history as we know it to a close and inaugurates a new age will God act decisively to restore . . . creation."—Paul J. Achtemeier, *Romans*, Interpretation, 8.

Overarching Themes

In the Old Testament four major concepts shape the way people think about God, about themselves, and about other people. Each concept influences our view of history and our understanding of Romans.

1. The *fall of Adam* introduces sin into the world. These words refer to the story of Eve and Adam eating the forbidden fruit and then hiding from God. Freedom is misused; punishment, fear, and alienation are the result.

2. *Covenant* is God's commitment to care for the world and the people in it. God comes to Abraham and Sarah and makes a covenant with them and with their descendants, including Abraham's son Ishmael. The sign of the covenant will be land, but the promise of covenant is blessing for all the peoples of the earth. Covenant gives human life dignity and worth, even when our own sin or the sins of others threaten to destroy us.

> "Paul is clear that since Adam the power to which creatures are subjected is sin."—Paul J. Achtemeier, *Romans*, Interpretation, 16.

3. *Law* is the expression of God's will for all of creation. The law of God is given to Moses on Mount Sinai. The first four command-

ments speak of our relationship with God; the last six speak of our relationship with people. The whole of the law reveals God's will for God's people.

4. The *future rule of God* is the conviction that sin cannot irreversibly alter God's purposes for creation. God's power to complete creation and God's commitment to bring blessing to the peoples of the earth will be realized when the rule of God brings about justice and righteousness for all people. We cannot discern the future rule of God on our own. The nature of God's rule must be revealed to us. The Greek word for "revelation" is *apokalypsis,* from which our English word "apocalypse" is derived. Writings that describe the future of creation as revealed by God are called "apocalyptic literature." The expectation of future fulfillment is called "apocalyptic expectation" (Achtemeier, 7–8).

For Paul, the gospel changes our understanding of all four ideas or concepts. The coming of Jesus and the establishment of the church occur in history. Yet these events lead us to look beyond history to a time of judgment and the establishment of a "new heaven and a new earth."

Out of the conviction that the coming of Jesus creates a new way to look at human affairs (history), Paul becomes a New Testament person. Here's his thinking: Adam brought sin into the world through failure to trust God and through disobedience, resulting in death. Christ brought trust, obedience, and life into the world, resulting in new life.

A Pauline diagram of God's activity in the world might look like this (from Achtemeier, 8):

Adam	Coming of Christ	Return of Christ
↓	↓	↓
sin	faith, hope, reconciliation, life	salvation, God's visible rule

The New Life in Christ

Within this understanding of God's active involvement with creation, faith is defined as joyous trust in the loving power of God. Faith becomes the means of seeing history as the arena in which

God brings blessing to creation. This understanding and perspective leads to *justification by faith,* a phrase we encounter in Romans.

For Paul, Abraham and Sarah are the first models for faith. They trust God, although they do not always obey God. Their descendants become the nation Israel. Israel does not always trust God, but God is always faithful to Israel. The church is seen as the new Abraham and Sarah and the new Israel.

The gospel is the good news that we are not prisoners to past unfaithfulness or to ourselves or to our own weaknesses. We are the loved children of our Creator, another way of expressing the Pauline understanding of *grace.* The love that comes to us from God, through Christ, leads us to be concerned with ethics and the law. Ethics and law cannot lead to love. But the love of God and the grace of God lead us to *want* to obey the law of God.

Ave Maria, by Horatio Walker (1903)

The crucifixion becomes for Paul a symbol of God's love and forgiveness. To recognize our need to be forgiven by God is *to be crucified with Christ.* To participate in the new life that comes by the spirit of God is *to be raised with Christ.* Resurrection becomes a symbol of the apocalyptic kingdom of God, as well as revelation of the power of God to make the symbol a reality.

As Paul becomes a "New Testament person," the language of the gospel story provides the framework through which he develops his theology. Theology is often defined as "faith seeking understanding." Paul has received the gift of faith; so, too, has the church. The church has grown in response to the gospel. The church transcends cultural and national barriers. The church overcomes ancient barriers of hostility and misunderstanding. Paul now seeks to examine this faith and to put into words the power of Christian faith for human life.

The letter to the Romans is not a formal textbook on theology, nor is it a letter in the usual sense of the word. Romans is a powerful reflection upon the gift of faith in God that comes through Jesus the Christ by the power of the Holy Spirit. Romans can perhaps be best compared to a magnificent piece of music, such as Handel's *Messiah*. *Messiah* draws heavily upon Old Testament themes as it tells the New Testament story. *Messiah* is often repetitive, yet it is also magnificent. It was dashed off in a relatively short time, yet it is complex and rich, and it endures. For most people, *Messiah* is a gift to hear, enjoy, and inspire. For music scholars, it is also a piece of music to be examined in depth.

Romans, like great music, is to be enjoyed. Treasure this letter as a gift from God that has enriched the church through the ages. Then examine the letter, seeking to understand what gives the letter its power to transform and to affirm faith in God.

Want to Know More?

About Paul? See C. K. Barrett, *Paul: An Introduction to His Thought* (Louisville Ky.: Westminster John Knox Press, 1994); Martin Hengel and Anna Maria Schwemer, *Paul between Damascus and Antioch* (Louisville, Ky.: Westminster John Knox Press, 1997); and Bruce J. Malina and Jerome H. Neyrey, *Portraits of Paul: An Archaeology of Ancient Personality* (Louisville, Ky.: Westminster John Knox Press, 1996).

About the use of the Old Testament in the New Testament? See Paul J. Achtemeier, ed., *Harper's Bible Dictionary* (San Francisco: Harper & Row, 1985), 723–27; also Leland Ryken et al., *Dictionary of Biblical Imagery* (Downers Grove, Ill.: InterVarsity Press, 1998), 90–92.

About the main characters in the book of Genesis? See Celia Brewer Marshall, *Genesis*, Interpretation Bible Studies (Louisville, Ky.: Geneva Press, 1999).

Questions for Reflection

1. Paul's context shaped the context of his letter to the Romans. What context shapes your receipt of this letter? What expectations and assumptions do you bring to Romans?
2. How does Paul's conviction that God acts through concrete events within the arena of human history lead Paul to wrestle with the experience of the Jews and the question of the Jews as God's chosen people?
3. Paul relies heavily on Old Testament imagery for his concepts of

law, sin, grace, and *righteousness.* What are some other biblical images that can build on these images?

4. This unit asserts that the biblical concept of *covenant* reveals God's commitment to care for the world and the people in it. *Covenant* gives human life dignity and worth, even when our sins or the sins of others threaten to destroy us. How do you respond to this assertion? What experiences or opinions do you have to support or refute the assertion?

Opening the Letter—Meeting the Author and Recipients

We know very little about the church in Rome. It may have been composed of several "house churches"; the membership may have included both converted Jews and Gentile Christians. From the book of Acts we know that Jews from Rome, along with proselytes (converted Jews), were present at the first Christian Pentecost (Acts 2:10). From references in the letter, we can conclude that Paul probably knew some of the Christians who lived in Rome. Perhaps he had met them in his travels to other churches. Perhaps members of other churches had moved to Rome and had become active in either starting or strengthening the church in that city.

> "All of his life Paul had been haunted by the thought of Rome. It had always been one of his dreams to preach there."—William Barclay, *The Letter to the Romans,* Daily Study Bible, 2.

Evidence within the letter would suggest that it was written toward the end of Paul's ministry, sometime between A.D. 55 and A.D. 64, perhaps while Paul was in Macedonia (Greece). Chapter 15 suggests that the letter may have been written in Corinth, near Athens, just prior to Paul's leaving for Jerusalem. If so, then the conflicts and struggles of the Corinthian church would have been much on Paul's mind as he wrote to the Romans.

As we read Romans, it may be helpful to imagine that we are sitting among the first recipients of the letter. Around us are people who have traveled widely; some are of Jewish background, others are Gentiles. Some may have positions in government or be professionals, such as teachers or doctors. Some will be parents; all will be children. Everyone present will have some sense of who "God" is, some understanding of "faith," and some desire to grow toward greater maturity as a person. Yet all will be different, and all will hear the letter from Paul in unique ways. The letter would have sparked much discussion among the first-century recipients, just as it will among readers in our own time.

Reading Romans brings rich rewards. The letter gives insight into the early days of the church. Although Paul did not know many of the Christians in Rome, he was writing to strangers who shared his faith. We may safely assume that the Roman community of faith was intelligent. The community members lived in a place of great power; they experienced many cultural pressures and influences which shaped their thinking. We cannot assume that the Romans heard Paul's words the same way we hear them. We cannot assume that the Romans looked for the same answers or affirmations in Paul's words that we might seek to find for our questions and concerns. Therefore, we read Romans not to hear Paul's words, but God's word to the church.

> "Within the biblical canon, the letter to the Romans has become a 'textbook' for the Christian faith."—Peter Stuhlmacher, *Paul's Letter to the Romans: A Commentary* (Louisville, Ky.: Westminster John Knox Press, 1994), 17.

> "Through the years, the whole church, and not just the Roman community of the first century, has heard Paul's words as addressed to us."—David L. Bartlett, *Romans,* Westminster Bible Companion, 15.

A Good Beginning (1:1–5)

As the letter opens, Paul introduces himself and gives his own sense of identity (1:1–2). Paul understands himself as a servant/slave of Jesus Christ. He has been called to be an apostle, set apart for the gospel of God. Throughout Romans, Paul emphasizes that Christian faith points us toward God, not to Jesus. Reflect on the significance of Pauline theology as "theocentric"; that is, "God centered." Romans challenges any faith that centers upon individual spiritual experience. One of the temptations in the Christian faith is to put so much emphasis on Jesus that God is squeezed out of our faith picture. Romans challenges the understanding of Christian faith that one need only "believe in Jesus" or "have a personal relationship with Jesus." This understanding falls short in at least two ways. First, it too easily presumes that we somehow *do* something and God through Jesus responds to us—that faith depends upon our initiative. Romans forces the reader to realize that faith begins with God. Second, Romans enlarges the scope of faith to show that the world is to trust God. The source of faith is not Jesus, but God. The God we meet in Jesus and come to know through Romans is not different from Jesus but is *much bigger* than Jesus.

In his excellent book *Transforming Mission,* David Bosch gives helpful insight into Paul's own introduction to the Christian faith. Bosch reports that some current scholars insist that Paul did not experience a "conversion" on the Damascus road. These scholars hold that conversion implies *changing from* one's religion to another. They hold that Paul's faith in God remained constant; his understanding of that faith and the power of that faith for his life were radically *transformed* by the Damascus road experience. A second reason these scholars advance for avoiding the term "conversion" is the implication that Paul was beset by deep guilt and great inner conflict prior to the encounter with the resurrected Christ.

"To all God's beloved in Rome."

Nothing in the writings of Paul indicates this to be true. The fourth century, with St. Augustine's *Confessions,* and the sixteenth century, with Martin Luther's deep personal struggles, introduced the western concept of conversion. They conclude that Paul's experience on the Damascus road might more properly be understood as a "call." The experience gave him his vocation; he became an apostle to the Gentiles.

Bosch rejects this challenge to the traditional term "conversion." He insists that Paul underwent a radical change in his values, in his self-definition, and in his commitments. Bosch argues that the term "conversion," or at least "transformation," does describe what happened to Paul. Of equal importance, Bosch says Paul understood his own experience to be a paradigm for every Christian. Peter, Paul, and John—all of whom had lived as righteous Jews—had to experience something else to be members of the people of God; they had to have faith in Christ. The Christ event signifies the reversal of the ages and denotes for Paul the proclamation of the new state of affairs that God has initiated in Christ (Bosch, 125–26).

After establishing his authority, Paul then summarizes the gospel (1:3–5). The gospel is a message concerning God's Son who is descended from David and declared to be the Son of God. These words point us to an important issue for the early church: the dual nature of Jesus' identity. Jesus is fully human, a descendant of King David and a Jew; Jesus is also fully divine, the Son of God.

"Paul is concerned with his apostolic commissioning with the gospel of Christ, which has been entrusted to him, and with the agreement of all Christians in Rome in regard to this gospel and Paul's apostolic office."—Peter Stuhlmacher, *Paul's Letter to the Romans: A Commentary* (Louisville, Ky.: Westminster John Knox Press, 1994), 19.

As Paul introduces the letter, he is asserting that the gospel is a proclamation of who we are created to become, a revelation of what it means to be fully and truly human. And the gospel is a revelation of who God is, of the essential nature and purpose of our Creator. Throughout Romans, Paul bestows great dignity upon human beings, as well as great glory upon God.

To complete his affirmations, Paul reminds the Romans that Jesus was raised with power (v. 4). God raised him to life through the power of the Holy Spirit. Then Paul speaks of the impact of Jesus upon Paul and upon the church. Jesus is the source of grace and apostleship; he brings about obedience of faith among the Gentiles.

Karl Barth says of this opening, "In this name [Jesus Christ], two planes intersect, the one known and the other unknown. The known plane is God's creation, fallen out of its union with Him, and therefore the world of the 'flesh,' needing redemption. This known plane is intersected by another plane that is unknown—the world of the Father, of the Primal Creation, and of the Final Redemption. . . . The point on the line of intersection at which the relation becomes observable and observed is Jesus, Jesus of Nazareth, the historical Jesus" (Barth, 29).

To My Friends (1:6-13)

After this carefully worded personal introduction and statement of faith, Paul addresses the Romans. Paul is writing to people who are also called to belong to Christ Jesus. Then he goes further; they are "called to be saints," which is a Pauline expression for those people who are Christians; "saints" is another word for disciples. In greeting the Romans, Paul uses the combination of *grace*, a Greek greeting, and *peace*, a Hebrew greeting. This combination of

"The apostle brings the gifts with which he is sent. The messenger declares the message with which he has been entrusted. Grace. Peace. Good news. Gospel."—David L. Bartlett, *Romans*, Westminster Bible Companion, 19.

words emphasizes the universality of the gospel. A prayer of thanksgiving, which is typical of Greek letters and a standard element in Paul's writings, follows the greeting.

Paul carefully establishes a relationship with his recipients. The opening is an expression of respect and mutuality. Paul wants to be perceived as friend more than as teacher. For him, the gospel creates a unity and a fellowship, a shared sense of identity. The gospel is more than knowledge; it has a power to forge friendships, even among people who do not personally know each other.

These opening verses set the tone for the entire letter. Paul is not writing as a religious philosopher. He is writing out of strong personal conviction, a conviction that is verified within history by the growth of the church and the power of the gospel to cross cultural barriers. Paul understands that he has been called by God to become a servant to people whom he once regarded as of no value. Though Paul is writing primarily to Gentiles, he establishes a strong link to the Old Testament and to the Jewish heritage. What God long ago foretold is now being fulfilled.

> "It is because it is God who promises, and God who fulfills in [God's] own time and in [God's] own way, that we have confidence that that promise will in fact be fulfilled. It is God's mercy that is reliable, not our response to it, or our acts in earning it."—Paul J. Achtemeier, *Romans*, Interpretation, 32.

The gospel is primarily about God. Jesus Christ is significant because Jesus reveals the righteousness of God. God does for creation that which is right. Jesus enables us to trust the "rightness of God." That is the gospel message. This gospel becomes the basis for Paul's missionary zeal and his evangelistic fervor. God can be trusted. Believe that God is righteous and your sins will be forgiven. Believe that God can be trusted as righteous, and everything in creation that creates guilt, alienation, separation, and fear will subside. Believe that God can be trusted as righteous, and the desire to rebel against God through disobedience will be transformed into radical respect for God's law and a deep yearning to live by that law.

Gospel Power (1:14–17)

In writing to the Romans, Paul is shifting the focus of his ministry from the Eastern part of the world toward the West. He is writing out of his own authority, confident that the Jewish perspective on history can have meaning to the Gentiles. Paul is confident, too, that the gospel will break down ancient barriers of hostility. The opening greeting expresses the joy Paul has for shared faith.

Now, in this passage, Paul establishes his indebtedness to Greeks and barbarians, as well as to his own Jewish heritage (1:14). Then he declares his excitement over proclaiming the gospel to the Romans (1:15). Barbarians were uncultured people of the day; they did not speak or think as the Greeks did. The Greeks were wise; the barbarians were not wise. Paul believes that all people can hear the gospel and respond, and in so doing give the gospel added power. Paul believes that the Gentile branch of Christianity proves the power of the gospel. Preaching to the Romans is an obligation, but it is also a privilege and a joy. As the gospel takes root in the lives of Gentiles, the power of the gospel is made known to everyone without regard to race or cultural heritage.

> "The letter is . . . very likely intended to lay the theological groundwork for Rome's support of [Paul's] mission to the western part of their world."—Paul J. Achtemeier, *Romans*, Interpretation, 29.

Paul's passion is to show the world that God is Lord of all, a passion reflected in 1:16-17. These verses are often seen as a statement giving the theme of Romans. The covenant first made with Abraham and Sarah is being fulfilled. "In Christ, God has remained faithful and true to his covenant promises and in that way has shown himself to be righteous" (Achtemeier, 37).

These verses emphasize the importance of the word *faith* for Paul and to any full understanding of Romans. We believe in the righteousness of God by faith, which in turn creates faith. Romans frequently uses the word *faith*, and on occasion seeks to define the word in objective terms. However, the great value of Romans is its ability to communicate a deeper, sacred meaning of the word *faith*, relying upon both the written words of the letter and the Spirit of God that moves upon readers of this letter.

📖 Want to Know More?

About house churches? See William H. Willimon, *Acts*, Interpretation (Atlanta: John Knox Press, 1988), 39–42; Carolyn Osiek and David L. Balch, *Families in the New Testament World: Households and House Churches* (Louisville, Ky.: Westminster John Knox Press, 1997). For the more contemporary movement of house churches, see J. G. Davies, ed., *The New Westminster Dictionary of Liturgy and Worship* (Philadelphia: Westminster Press, 1986), 260–62.

About the concept of call? See Alan Richardson and John Bowden, eds., *The Westminster Dictionary of Christian Theology* (Philadelphia: Westminster Press, 1983), 79.

In the letter to the Romans, which is the only letter written to a church he did not personally establish, Paul reveals that the gospel has given him a new worldview. Paul's theology and his understanding of mission do not simply relate to each other as "theory" on the one hand and as "practice" on the other. Rather, Paul is showing how his theology is a missionary theology. His understanding of the gospel is dependent on the faith of others, not just on his own experience or insight. Missionary activity is not something Christians do to share the gospel. Missionary activity is something Christians do to experience the full power of the gospel (Bosch, 124).

? Questions for Reflection

1. If you were asked to write down your understanding of Christian faith, what would you write? (If you have time, write down your understanding and save your response for comparison later in this study.)
2. This unit states that Paul's theology points to God, not to Jesus, and challenges a faith that focuses upon Jesus rather than God. What specific passages from this unit support or refute the statement? Do you agree or disagree with this statement? Why?
3. This unit claims that "Jesus enables us to trust the 'rightness of God.' That is the gospel message." What is the "rightness of God"? What are your thoughts on this subject?
4. What are some ways one can experience the power of the gospel?

3 Romans 1:18–2:16

Sin and Salvation

Paul begins to share both the struggle and the joy of the gospel. This section is crucial to understanding Romans. Paul is diagnosing the tragic dimension of the human life called sin. When we trust God, we turn away from lesser gods. When we do not trust God, we remove ourselves from fellowship with God, a stance that leads to destruction. For Paul, sin leads to the wrath of God. The *wrath of God* may perhaps best be understood as "God's steadfast and holy hatred of sin" (*Oxford Annotated Bible, NRSV,* Colossians 3:6, note). Wrath is the divine consequence of rebellion and self-deception. Wrath is not so much intentionally inflicted upon us by God as it is a divinely ordained result of our sin (1:18).

> "Wrath is itself finally a servant of the gracious purpose of God to restore [God's] lordship over [a] rebellious creation."—Paul J. Achtemeier, *Romans,* Interpretation, 48.

The Many Faces of Sin
—Part I (1:18–32)

Paul asserts that all people, even apart from the revelation of God in the law and through Christ, have the possibility of knowing the likelihood of the punishment that comes from sin. This creates a natural fear of God. Instead of seeking to know God's will, which is merciful, people have rebelled against God even more (1:19–22).

Verse 22 is a definition of sin: "Claiming to be wise, they became fools." Adam and Eve thought that by eating the forbidden fruit they would become wise like God. Human beings, endowed with limited

20

free will, continue to fall into the same trap. For Paul, to be a human being is to be a creature, dependent upon one's Creator. Rather than joyfully accepting our status as creatures, we proceed to claim to be wiser than we are; we proceed to structure life on our own terms. We trust our wisdom more than we trust God's will and God's ways.

The nature of sin is the same in the twentieth century as the first— relying on some idol, often the idol of self, instead of on God. Think about the foolish things on which we rely to give us power and importance. Reflect upon the ways we follow our own inclinations, calling them true, when in fact we know that God's truth runs counter to our own version of truth. Paul uses the image of four-footed reptiles and animals, probably a reference to specific idols of the first century. Compare that image

The subtle temptation of idolatry is to place our confidence in that which is not God.

with the trust we place in four-wheel-drive vehicles, which give us the illusion of freedom to go anywhere, under all weather conditions, and which also symbolize our desire to escape pressure and to create security (1:23).

Lies, Lies, and More Lies

In verse 25 Paul gives a second definition of sin when he asserts that the unrighteous "exchanged the truth about God for a lie and worshiped and served the creature rather than the Creator." When we exchange the truth about God for a lie and worship and serve the creature rather than the Creator (1:25), we become prisoners to degrading passions. Sexual sins are listed (1:27); "every kind of wickedness" is then listed (1:28–31). The wrath of God occurs as God simply gives us up or allows us (1:26–28) to have our own way. God does not judge us from on high. God allows our own self-idolatry to judge us. Sin produces its own consequences and its own punishment.

Paul's definitions of sin point us back to the story of the serpent's encounter with Eve and Adam. That ancient Genesis story shows how humans may rationalize fulfilling our own desires, but we cannot change the truth. The truth is that when we put our own yearnings and passions first, we create havoc in our lives, and worse, we create havoc in the life of God's creation for generations to come.

> "If our goals are set with no final regard for the will of the true God as expressed in Jesus Christ, is it any wonder that we become less than we as human beings made in God's image ought to be?"—Paul J. Achtemeier, *Romans,* Interpretation, 38.

Paul makes two important points in these verses. First, God is worthy of our trust. God is righteous. God keeps promises (1:16–17). This is the gospel. Second, God is faithful to those promises; the "righteousness" of God is not something to be trifled with. To abuse God's offer of salvation and to imagine that God is something other than sovereign Lord and sole Creator brings terrible consequences (Achtemeier, 36–37).

An Order to the World

Paul's heritage from the Old Testament prophets convinced him that God has ordered the world in such a way that we ignore the laws of God at our own peril and at great cost to the whole of creation. Structural engineers have the freedom to ignore the laws of physics, but such ignorance results in bridges that collapse, often at the cost of innocent lives. God wills that the engineers have freedom; God wills that the laws of physics stand firm. God does not will that engineers ignore the laws of physics or that a particular individual will be on the bridge at the moment of collapse. The same analogy can be applied in many areas of life. When developers ignore the laws of ecology, many people suffer. When individuals ignore the laws of nutrition or morality, disease—both physical and social disease—is the result. The results of sin do not always directly affect the guilty individuals or the guilty social group; creation as a whole suffers.

To construct a bridge and ignore the laws of physics would have dangerous consequences.

This understanding of sin and the consequences of sin may catch some readers by surprise. However, it has deep biblical roots. Sin is rebellion and pride. Sin is trusting our own emotions, insights, and desires rather than trusting God's way and God's will. The punishment of sin is getting what we desire. However, sin ends up punishing not only us but all of creation, for when we rebel against God our misuse of freedom disturbs and distorts all of creation.

Because the human actions in Romans 1 are so often cited in crusades against immorality, this section is likely to spark discussion. As you read this chapter, realize that Paul is not seeking to give a list of sins. He is sharing his insight into the nature of sin. This discussion continues into the next chapter of the letter. To read chapter 1 of Romans apart from chapter 2 is to fall into a trap, the trap of believing ourselves wise, even wise about the ways of God, only to discover that we have become fools.

Idolatry Is the Issue

Chapter 1 makes the most specific reference to homosexuality in the New Testament. Scholars debate the exact meaning of "homosexuality" in the first century, inasmuch as the word itself was unknown. We cannot be sure of the exact description of the practices about which Paul is speaking. However, the central focus is clear: In any sphere of life or relationships, when we claim to be wise, we become fools. "Claiming to be wise" may include approval of sexual practices we enjoy for a time but which have traditionally been forbidden by the law and which eventually prove to be harmful to us as children of God. Or, as chapter 2 will affirm, "claiming to be wise" may refer to a passionate need to judge others, which leads only to alienation and hostility. When people in any one time or place "claim to be wise," including when we claim to know which passages of the Bible are most important, or when we assert that we know exactly what specific passages mean, time and *the wrath of God* of will show us to be fools.

Paul had a decidedly negative view toward the moral standards of Gentiles, a view that was common among Jewish people. However, immorality is not the primary target of Paul's concern. Immorality is a form of idolatry, as is trust in the law. Idols are fabrications of

> "I no longer think idolatry is a problem of primitive people in a simpler time, those who worshipped golden calves in fertility rites. I have only to open a newspaper to contemplate the wondrously various ways in which idolatry is alive in the here and now."—Kathleen Norris, *Amazing Grace: A Vocabulary of Faith* (New York: Riverhead Books, 1998), 92.

perverted human minds. Over against the pervasive idolatry of the Greco-Roman world, Paul proclaims an uncompromising message of God's exclusive claim upon human loyalty. For Paul, humanity apart from Christ is utterly lost. However, Paul's primary concern is not the "wrath to come." His message is more positive. Paul proclaims salvation through Christ and the imminent triumph of God. His gospel is *good news.* Paul proclaims the gospel not so much to "bring salvation" as to glorify God. Through God salvation comes to all people who experience transformation of life through the gospel (Bosch, 134–35).

The Many Faces of Sin —Part II (2:1–11)

The warnings in the last verses of chapter 1 lead directly into the opening verses of chapter 2. Chapter 1 of Romans focuses upon self-idolatry that ignores God and follows its own desires. Chapter 2 of the letter asserts that another form of self-idolatry is the inclination to judge others (2:1). Paul is clear: The will of God is not that we are to judge others; rather, we are to seek good (2:7). "Doers of the law will be justified" (2:13). However, obeying the law now becomes an inward obedience, "a matter of the heart" (2:29). Our calling is to hear the gospel and to build up the church, not to interpret the law.

Martin Luther captured an insight from Romans when he defined sin as "the heart turned in upon itself, the heart that enthrones itself in God's place." Notice how both the sins at the end of chapter 1 and sin as described in the opening verses of chapter 2 are manifestations of "the heart turned in upon itself."

C. K. Barrett, a noted British biblical scholar, says that this is a difficult passage. He suggests that the main points to grasp are these: (1) Human beings are God's creatures and are called to recognize our Creator as Lord and to love, honor, and trust God. (2) The fundamental human fault is to put ourselves in God's place. (3) This fault results sometimes in an immoral life, sometimes in a life of arrogant religiosity. Both are equally blameworthy. (4) The human conscience accuses the self; the only way to escape the wrath of God is the way of hope and faith (Barrett, 8–9).

> "In this passage we are face to face with the fact that the essence of sin is to put self in the place of God."—William Barclay, *Letter to the Romans,* Daily Study Bible, 28.

Connecting the First
Two Chapters of Romans

The relationship of chapter 1:18–32 to chapter 2:1–11 is crucial to understanding Paul. In current debates about issues of morality, Paul's opposition to the "sins of the flesh" as listed in chapter 1 is often cited. The sins of excessive religiosity in chapter 2 are often overlooked. A careful reading of Paul quickly silences those who would use Paul to judge people engaged in immoral actions. Paul does not advocate or encourage any type of sexual or ethical behavior that is contrary to the law of God; however, he refuses to advocate or encourage any effort to classify those sins as greater than the sins of mean-spiritedness, condemnation of others, or faultfinding.

A thoughtful reader may wonder if perhaps Paul is preaching to himself in the second chapter, remembering the zeal with which he persecuted the church and the quickness with which he found fault with those who did not practice the faith of the Pharisees. Certainly anyone who treasures the Christian life, is a strong member of a church, and is a recognized Christian will have to ask whether or not the sins of chapter 2 have caused separation from God and alienation from other people and thereby become a barrier to effective proclamation of the gospel.

> "Idolatry is the practice of ascribing absolute value to things of relative worth."—Frederick Buechner, *Wishful Thinking: A Theological ABC* (New York: Harper & Row, 1973), 40.

Students of this passage will find it important to remember that when Paul uses the words *the law,* he is referring to the Jewish law of Moses, specifically the Ten Commandments given on Mount Sinai, the law that later came to include the rite of circumcision. Long after Moses and the wilderness experience, Old Testament law led to the development of Rabbinic Judaism and to the Jewish sect known as Pharisees. Paul had been a Pharisee (Acts 22:3; Philippians 3:5–6). Paul understood *law* to be the Old Testament expression of God's will (Buttrick, 774–81). Paul treasures the law of Moses; he does not treasure the intricate interpretations of the law by the Pharisees and the resulting burden those interpretations place upon people.

When referring to Gentiles, *the law* refers to the "law of conscience," or "natural law" (2:14).

Faith and Law in Tension

The relationship between faith and law is a major topic for Paul and for the church throughout the centuries. Pay careful attention to this section. On the one hand, if we rely upon the law for our own righteousness, or if we use the law to determine the righteousness of others, we are failing to hear the gospel. On the other hand, if we think we can ignore the law and trust our faith in God alone, then we are making ourselves into God.

Central to Paul's concern is his own personal awareness that the law can make a person impatient and unkind. God's very nature causes God to be rich in kindness, forbearance, and patience (2:4). When we grasp the righteousness of God, we ourselves become righteous in our attitude toward others. God's kindness is a means of evangelism (2:4). God's kindness is toward the Jews and toward the Gentiles.

With this section, Paul begins a subtle shift that will soon dominate much of the letter. Paul has a passion for the Gentiles to hear the gospel and to respond, but he has a equal passion to remind the Gentile Christians that God can be kind also to the Jews. God shows no partiality (2:11).

Paul affirms that all who have sinned apart from the law will perish apart from the law, and all who have sinned under the law will be judged by the law. Gentiles may instinctively obey the law and thereby become a law unto themselves. In a confusing sentence, Paul concludes that this action may or may not accuse or excuse them from judgment. The point Paul is making is that anyone may obey the law, but such obedience may turn into a form of self-righteousness and a judgmental spirit, which then will be a cause for condemnation.

Want to Know More?

About the wrath of God? See Leland Ryken et al., *Dictionary of Biblical Imagery* (Downers Grove, Ill.: InterVarsity Press, 1998), 25–26.

About sin? See Shirley C. Guthrie, *Christian Doctrine*, rev. ed. (Louisville, Ky.: Westminster John Knox Press, 1994), 212–27.

About the Bible and homosexuality? For a survey of the variety of views on this subject, see Stanley J. Grenz, *Welcoming but Not Affirming: An Evangelical Response to Homosexuality* (Louisville, Ky.: Westminster John Knox Press, 1998), 35–62; Marion L. Soards, *Scripture & Homosexuality: Biblical Authority and the Church Today* (Louisville, Ky.: Westminster John Knox Press, 1995), 15–29; and Jeffrey S. Siker, *Homosexuality in the Church: Both Sides of the Debate* (Louisville, Ky.: Westminster John Knox Press, 1994), 3–35. For related discussions, see Robert L. Brawley, *Biblical Ethics and Homosexualty* (Louisville, Ky.: Westminster John Knox Press, 1996) and Choon-Leong Seow, ed., *Homosexuality and Christian Community* (Louisville, Ky.: Westminster John Knox Press, 1996).

? Questions for Reflection:

1. What evidence do you see in contemporary life that sin produces its own consequences and punishment and that the wrath of God is the consequence of God allowing us to have our own way?
2. Reflect on Paul's image for sin as claiming to be wise while in fact becoming fools. What are the sources of wisdom?
3. How does the description or definition of sin in question 2 apply to sexual behavior? How does it apply to judging or condemning others? How is immorality a form of idolatry? How can condemning others be a form of idolatry?
4. What are some of the lies which have been exchanged for truth? How does a lie become accepted as truth?

Faith as "Trust" versus Belief or Obedience

Any discussion of *faith* for Paul involves wrestling with God's relationship to the Jewish people. In the Bible, faith begins when God calls Abram and Sarai, and they go forth toward the land God has promised them. Paul has put himself into a difficult predicament. Since God called the Jewish people into covenant and gave them the law, Paul's arguments can be heard as discounting the value of being a Jew. Nevertheless, Paul believes that being a Jew is an advantage over being a Gentile. Jews are the ones to whom God has communicated, who know who God is. The Jew has the "oracles of God" (3:2), the Hebrew Bible or Old Testament. Although the Old Testament law condemns all, the Old Testament also bears witness to God's faithful love and covenant promises.

> "Paul here singles out the Jews precisely because their status as chosen people could have tempted one to assume they were exempt from the wrath of God about which Paul has been speaking."—Paul J. Achtemeier, *Romans,* Interpretation, 50.

Christianity and the Jews (2:17–3:20)

Paul's introduces his concern for the Jews in the previous section, at chapter 2, verse 10; the concern accelerates in verses 17–29, and then becomes the focus of the opening verses of chapter 3. The main points are these: (1) The Jews are the chosen people of God (1:16; 3:2). (2) To be chosen is not to be exempted from God's wrath (2:9, 17–24).

(3) "Chosenness" is not a matter of outward marks but rather an inner reality (2:25–29). (4) To be "chosen" is to be chosen to serve God concretely in one's life, not to be granted immunity from God's wrath. (5) Yet God will remain faithful to the covenant promises (3:4).

> "To be shown favor by God does not absolve one from responsibility; rather it confers responsibility upon one."—Paul J. Achtemeier, *Romans*, Interpretation, 52.

Therefore, Jews have the law and "all the law does is to tell us what is sinful" (Romans 3:20, Jerusalem Bible). Christians have Christ, who confirms the righteousness of God, thereby creating in us faith. Faith in the righteousness of God becomes both a promise of forgiveness and a call to greater obedience and service. To claim the law as a vehicle for our own righteousness is only to be deluded and trapped by sin. To live by the grace of God, which engenders faith, is to be set free from believing we can obey the law. Yet to live by the grace of God is to become respectful of the law, because the law is the will of God.

Paul is making a dramatic shift away from religious observance of law, which is always open to perversion and abuse, toward a *faith* relationship between God and people. This relationship is based not upon obedience but upon a humble, believing dependence upon God. Paul's concern for the Jews points to the distinction that is often made between "religion" and "faith." Religion is any human effort to be reconciled to God through acts of piety and virtue. Faith is trusting the love, will, and justice of God, no matter how failed or flawed we may be (Barrett, 12–13).

The Law of Faith (3:21–31)

This passage reveals a significant shift in Paul's message. Instead of accentuating the negative aspects of law, wrath, and sin, Paul begins to explain *faith*. Some biblical scholars point out that the Greek preposition connected to the word "faith" can be translated "of" as well as "in." Therefore, verse 22 and other similar verses may be translated "through faith in Jesus Christ," or "through the faith of Jesus Christ." The two possible translations are complementary. Paul connects the righteousness of God with the faith *of* Jesus as well as faith *in* Jesus (3:22, 26). The gospel leads to faith in God that comes, not through the law of Moses, but through the faith of Jesus. Jesus trusted God; Jesus obeyed God. Though Jesus was crucified because of his trust in

God, God raised Jesus from the dead, thereby vindicating Jesus' trust in God and vindicating God. God's power to restore life and to restore fellowship with those from whom Jesus had been alienated is now revealed.

One helpful way of wrestling with the definition of *faith* is to realize that genuine faith begins with Jesus. For Christians, to profess "faith *in* Jesus" includes meaning we believe in Jesus' revelation of faith. Christians don't just believe in Jesus as Lord and Savior. We believe in trusting and obeying God the way Jesus trusted and obeyed God. The faith of Jesus reveals two great truths about God: First, God loves the world so much, God is willing to become incarnate, to suffer and die so that the world might know of the greatness of God's love. Christians call this sacrificial death *atonement* (3:25). Second, because of the revelation that occurs through Jesus, Christians believe that God's love and God's power are victorious over every power that seeks to defeat us, including the self-centeredness of betrayal, denial, and death.

> "By living out [Jesus'] faith in God in our own lives we accept that righteousness which God does through him and his obedience. . . . Faith is our response to God's making us right in Jesus Christ."—David L. Bartlett, *Romans*, Westminster Bible Companion, 38.

These truths empower all people to trust God, which gives the gospel universal power. Because of Jesus, through the proclamation of the gospel, there is no distinction. All people can trust God; all people will have to trust God if they are to be in right relationship with God. Acceptance of "God as God" is what Paul calls the *law of faith* (3:27). We become righteous because we trust God, not because we can obey God. We no longer need to or seek to prove our worth; our worth comes through God's love for us and God's gracious care toward us (3:30).

> "However faithless humanity may prove to be, God remains faithful."—Paul J. Achtemeier, *Romans*, Interpretation, 55.

Paul concludes with an important and often repeated theme: The faith in God that comes through Jesus does not overthrow the law; this faith seeks to uphold the law (3:31). Because we trust God, God's law is worthy of our respect. Faith in God puts law on a "firmer footing" (Romans 3:31, New English Bible).

This theme of faith and law is essential to Paul's message in Romans, but the concept is confusing. Paul Tillich's insights may be helpful. Tillich, a German scholar who came to the United States to flee the Nazis, writes of three types of law: autonomy, heteronomy, theonomy. Autonomy is literally "self-law." This is the basic human position toward law. This position contends, "I know what is best for my life. I establish what rules should be obeyed and which rules can be ignored." Into this situation of self-confidence comes heteronomy, or "opposite law." Heteronomy is law that opposes my will, using the promise of reward or the threat of punishment to coerce me into obedience. The higher alternative is theonomy, which is God's law.

What is our attitude toward the law?

A helpful way of relating these three attitudes toward the law is to think of the way many people determine the "right speed" on the highway. Under normal circumstances, many decide the "right speed" is that which allows for a safe and timely trip. That is an autonomous approach. However, introducing the appearance of a highway patrol car creates the heteronomous approach. Fear of punishment creates obedience to an outside authority, in this case, the posted speed limit. Theonomy occurs when the driver is personally convinced that the posted speed limit is the fastest and safest rate of speed, and so obedience becomes both voluntary and desired. The trip is made not out of guilt or anxiety, but instead in peace.

Faith in God's righteousness creates a similar response in our lives. When we trust God's righteousness, we trust God's wisdom and God's goodness; therefore we want to obey God's law. God's law becomes the desire of our lives. God's law replaces self-law, but not out of fear of punishment or desire for reward. *The replacement occurs out of gratitude, trust, and respect* (Tillich, 83–86).

John Calvin, in his *Institutes of the Christian Religion*, gives three uses of the law for Christian people:

a. The law convicts everyone of unrighteousness and opens all to the need for God's grace (Romans 3:20).

32

   b. The law protects the community from the unjust, serving as a deterrent to those who are not yet regenerate.

   c. The law admonishes believers and shows them the right things to do.

Though a devout advocate of the grace of God, Calvin strongly believed that the law of God has a clear and vital purpose within the Christian community (Calvin, *Institutes*, 354–64).

Thoughtful readers of Romans will want to reflect on the place the law has in human life. Our understanding of the role of law changes as we mature both as individuals who live in a secular society and as people of faith. Law can help prevent destructive behavior, but law can never make a person "good." A person's growth in character and integrity transcends obedience to the law. Strengthening this capacity for transcendence is part of the power of the gospel.

> **Want to Know More?**
>
> **About chosenness or election?** See Paul J. Achtemeier, ed., *Harper's Bible Dictionary* (San Francisco: Harper, 1985), 254.
>
> **About faith?** See Thomas G. Long, *Hebrews*, Interpretation (Louisville, Ky.: John Knox Press, 1997), 113–15.
>
> **About atonement?** See Shirley C. Guthrie, *Christian Doctrine*, rev. ed. (Louisville, Ky.: Westminster John Knox Press, 1994), 250–69.

Abraham as the "Father of Faith" (4:1–25)

Paul shifts again to Abraham as a model of faith. Abraham "believed God." This "trust in him who justifies the ungodly" is called "faith" (4:5); "such faith is reckoned as righteousness" (see Gen. 15:6). Paul also makes a reference to David, specifically to David's sin with Bathsheba. However, Abraham is the primary focus. Paul's second point in using Abraham as an example is that circumcision came *after* faith, as a sign *of* faith, not as a precondition to faith. Abraham remains a key figure in Paul's understanding of gospel. God blessed Abraham and Sarah before they had done anything to deserve blessing, and God continued to bless them even after acts of disobedience (Achtemeier, 79).

Paul's point, which is essential to an understanding of Romans, is that (a) faith in God rests upon our confidence in God's grace (4:16), which leads to *hope,* and (b) to grow "strong in . . . faith" is "being fully convinced that God [is] able to do what [God has] promised" (4:21).

Paul does not refer to Abraham's lack of trust, either in passing

Sarah off as his sister or in the birth of Ishmael. However, these events in Abraham's life would only reinforce his position. Abraham's righteousness does not make him a person of strong faith; Abraham's trust in the righteousness of God and the trustworthy nature of God's promises makes Abraham "the father of the faithful."

Therefore at 4:22 leads into a discussion of the word "reckoned." This verse creates a shift away from past faith history toward present experience of faith. At 4:23, Paul says that the true contemporary descendants of Abraham are those who trust in God through the revelation of God's righteousness made known in the faith of Jesus and the life, death, and resurrection of Jesus (4:24–25). Those who trust in the revelation of God's righteousness become righteous after the manner of Abraham. Abraham is vindicated not only by the gospel but also by the whole Old Testament. Old Testament law, rightly understood, is confirmed by the gospel (Barrett, 21).

> "One becomes a descendant of Abraham, in Paul's view, only by sharing his trust, not his genes."—Paul J. Achtemeier, *Romans*, Interpretation, 79.

This portion of Romans and the chapters that follow were a major influence in shaping the faith of those who brought about the Protestant Reformation. A study of the history of the Reformation makes us aware that without Romans, the Reformation probably would never have occurred. Prior to the Protestant Reformation, Martin Luther wrote:

"The just shall live by faith"—the gate to heaven

I greatly longed to understand Paul's Epistle to the Romans and nothing stood in the way except that one expression, "the justice of God," because I took it to mean that justice whereby God is just and deals justly in punishing the unjust. My situation was just that, although an impeccable monk, I stood before God as a sinner troubled in conscience, and I had no confidence that my merit would assuage him. Therefore, I did not love a just and angry God, but rather hated and murmured against him. Yet I clung to that dear Paul and had a great yearning to know what he meant.

Night and day, I pondered until I saw the connection between the justice of God and the statement that "the just shall live by his faith." Then I grasped that the justice of God is that righteousness by which through grace and sheer mercy God justifies us through faith. Thereupon I felt myself to be reborn and to have gone through open doors into paradise. The whole of scripture took on a new meaning, and whereas before the phrase the "justice of God" had filled me with hate, now it became to me inexpressibly sweet in greater love. This passage of Paul became to me a gate to heaven. (Bainton, 65)

? Questions for Reflection

1. Notice how Paul raises a question, sometimes an objection, then proceeds to answer his own argument. This appears to be a common style of the day, dating back to Plato and Socrates. The purpose of the style is more educational than argumentative (Achtemeier, 73–76). How effective is this "dialogical style" in the teaching of this letter?
2. God has accepted us in Christ. How does understanding God's acceptance affect the way we view the world and others?
3. What are some of the ways our culture offers people opportunities to prove their worth and achieve security through their own efforts? How do these cultural temptations make it hard to accept grace?
4. Paul acknowledges that for Abraham it was unlikely that God could do what God had promised (4:19), yet Abraham was "fully convinced that God was able to do what he had promised" (4:21). Does Abraham's involvement with Hagar, although encouraged by Sarah, represent a contradiction to Paul's assertion of "fully convinced"? What situations or circumstances today make trusting God's promises seem foolish? How is Abraham an example for Christians in our day?

5 Romans 5:1–6:23

Justified, Reconciled, Sanctified

Teachers of Romans always alert students to notice the word *therefore,* which occurs frequently in this epistle. Wise advice is that when the word "therefore" appears in a Pauline letter, stop, look, and discover what the "therefore" is there for. This passage begins with the words, "Therefore, since we are justified by faith . . . " Let us stop, look, and discover the previous message upon which this passage is based.

The Backward Glance of Faith (5:1–5)

The genuine meaning of faith often comes by looking back over our lives and seeing the presence of God. The popular poem "Footprints," often sold in poster shops, captures this Pauline understanding of faith. When we look back to chapter 4 of Romans, we are reminded that faith comes to us through Jesus. Faith is not only believing in Jesus as Lord and Savior, but faith is also receiving the faith of Jesus, which enables us to trust in God every step of our journey. The faith of Jesus leads us to trust the ways and will of God, whether the meaning of the journey is clear or not. Such an understanding of faith involves trust and obedience as well as acceptance and confidence.

Faith trusts even when the journey is unclear.

The faith of Jesus allows us to know that God has faith *in us,* even when our faith *in God* is weak. Jesus could affirm that Peter would be the rock upon which Jesus would build his church (Matt. 16:18), even though Peter would deny that he ever even knew Jesus. The author of the First Letter of John affirms, "In this is love, not that we loved God but that he loved us and sent his Son to be the atoning sacrifice for our sins" (1 John 4:10). The *therefore* refers to Abraham's faith, which was a trust in the promises of God, not a confidence in Abraham's faith. The *therefore* also refers to belief in *him* (God) who raised Jesus from the dead, remembering that Jesus "was handed over to death for our trespasses and was raised for our justification" (Rom. 4:25). It is God's faith in us and God's love toward us that creates the gift Paul describes as *justification.* The conviction that we are justified by God's faith in us and God's love toward us creates peace with God.

> "We praise God not to celebrate our own faith but to give thanks for the faith God has in us."—Kathleen Norris, *Amazing Grace: A Vocabulary of Faith* (New York: Riverhead Books, 1998), 151.

Radical Acceptance

Justified and *justification* are Pauline words that have become important to our Protestant heritage. To be justified is to be made righteous (right), to be cleared of guilt. In the Middle Ages, printing was developed about the same time that the Protestant Reformation occurred; *justified* is the term used to describe the process by which type is lined up correctly. Even in our modern word processors, it is with the touch of a button that margins are evened out and the type lines up right where it should be.

The faith that leads to justification is confidence in God's righteousness; that is, God's power and God's love for all of creation as revealed by Jesus. This faith then leads to confidence in God's grace, which is the conviction that God is for us and not against us—even though God is firmly against sin!

Justification through this faith leads to peace with God. Out of both the convictions of this faith and the joy of this peace, we know and proclaim Jesus to be Lord of our lives and Lord of all creation, and the Christ, the promised Messiah sent by God.

The "glory of God" (5:2) of which we boast is the glorious conviction that God's love and power will bring upon the whole world the blessing that God first promised to Abraham and Sarah and all their descendants. As God fulfills this ancient covenant, we will share in God's glory, because we have foreseen this fulfillment and find peace through that promise. In that fulfillment we also will be blessed and fulfilled.

Martin Luther related the righteousness of God to the mercy of God, which leads to "radical acceptance," enabling humans to overcome the despair created by guilt (Harvey, 136–37).

In our time, the great manifestation of sin may not be despair over guilt as much as it is cynicism and nihilism—the question whether life has ultimate value and purpose. In our time, "justification" relates to the righteousness of God by asserting that life does have value, and creation will be fulfilled. These are bold statements in light of the persistence of chaos and suffering in the world.

After establishing a joyful affirmation of peace and grace in the opening verses of this chapter, Paul moves to place that affirmation within a theological framework by establishing how grace overcomes sin. For Paul, until one is convinced of the persistent power of sin, one cannot fully rejoice in the gift of grace. Sin alienates and convicts; grace reconciles and redeems. A proper understanding of sin and grace then leads to hope.

Want to Know More?

About hope? See John H. Leith, *Basic Christian Doctrine* (Louisville, Ky.: Westminster John Knox Press, 1993), 286–303. For a more detailed discussion, see Jürgen Moltmann, *Theology of Hope* (Minneapolis: Fortress Press, 1993).

About evil and suffering? See Shirley C. Guthrie, *Christian Doctrine*, rev. ed. (Louisville, Ky.: Westminster John Knox Press, 1994), 166–91; Tyron L. Inbody, *The Transforming God: An Interpretation of Suffering and Evil* (Louisville, Ky.: Westminster John Knox Press, 1997).

In the Face of Adversity

Hope was previously introduced in the last chapter in reference to Abraham (4:18–21). Faith in God that rests upon God's grace and not our own righteousness leads to hope. To "grow strong in faith" (4:20) is "being fully convinced that God is able to do what God has promised" (4:21).

Paul is realistic about the enemies of faith. Achtemeier speaks of verses 3–5 as "confidence in the face of adverse reality" (Achtemeier, 91). The recognition of "adverse reality" is part of what makes Romans so powerful. God's grace is such that even things that work against confidence and hope serve to strengthen them. Paul starts with the reality of suffering. Yet the revelation of God that comes to us through Christ actually enables us to boast of our sufferings. We see in Christ the way in which suffering produces endurance, and endurance can create character, and character leads to hope—a hope not in our own strength or in our own righteousness. Rather, it is a hope that comes through confidence in God's love, a confidence that is "poured into our hearts through the Holy Spirit" (5:5).

The story is told about the relationship between a parent and a child. One evening, the child was arrested for driving recklessly in a car with other youths. The parents were heartbroken but supported their child through the shame and rehabilitation process. The child eventually matured and grew to be a police officer. Years later, upon reflecting on that incident, the child revealed that the actual driver of the car was another youth. The two had switched places before the officer got to the car. The parents could not understand the switch. "Why would you do such a thing?" they asked. The grown child replied, "Even though I knew it would hurt you very much, I knew that you loved me and wouldn't desert me. I couldn't say the same for his parents."

Perhaps this story suggests many things about friendship, sacrifice, and families, some of which may not be things we want to hear. But one of its good suggestions is that the confidence instilled by an unshakeable love can empower an individual to face great adversity.

Honest students of this passage will have to examine their own convictions about suffering, faith, and God. Suffering, especially undeserved suffering (such as that experienced by a child born into relentless poverty or brutal abuse), challenges faith in God. However, the affirmation of the power of faith to endure suffering with hope has been powerfully reaffirmed in our own century. The writings of Viktor Frankl, a Jew, affirm the power of faith, hope, and love to equip people to endure the Holocaust (*Man's Search for Meaning;* New York: Washington Square Press, 1984). Confidence in God's love toward us has equipped people to endure oppression and suffering, even to sacrifice their lives for justice and righteousness. The power of faith to equip people to oppose oppression, even at the risk of one's own life, is what Dietrich Bonhoeffer calls "the cost of discipleship." The grace of God does not allow us to accept sin; it empowers us to oppose sin in whatever form sin occurs. Bonhoeffer was much influenced by Romans.

Beyond Sin toward Salvation (5:6–21)

This section opens with an eloquent statement about the unmerited nature of God's love. The key words are "reconciled" and "reconciliation."

For Paul, *reconciliation* means moving beyond guilt and loneliness through the love and forgiveness of God. Note that "we were reconciled to God through the death of his Son, . . . [we will] be saved by his life" (v. 10), not by our faith.

> "The melancholy fact is . . ., humans as a race repeat the sin of their original "ancestor."—Paul J. Achtemeier, *Romans*, Interpretation, 96.

Paul then speaks of the power of sin, as it existed from Adam to Moses. In Paul's argumentation, Adam destined all to sin. The abundance of grace and the "free gift" of righteousness that leads to justification is now available to all through Christ (5:12–21). "Christ got us out of the mess Adam got us into" (Achtemeier, 97).

Adam and Christ represent a dichotomy: Adam—death, chaos, a cosmic order gone awry; Christ—abundant grace, cosmic victory, God's righteousness that can set all creation right. "By undoing, through obedience, what Adam did by disobedience, Christ turns humanity in a new direction" (Achtemeier, 99). This passage is a primary source for the doctrine of "original sin."

> "The larger dimension of Paul's thought . . . becomes evident here, with Adam and Christ pointing to the two possible fates of humanity—sin leading to death and grace leading to life."—Paul J. Achtemeier, *Romans*, Interpretation, 99.

Note the *therefore* at 5:12 and 5:18. Achtemeier stresses that this passage shows that when "sinners 'try harder,' they only produce more sin. The deeper element of self-examination is the need to repent of the feeling that by 'trying harder' we can effect reconciliation with God. That (feeling) is simply another form of the temptation to 'be like God' that was the downfall of Eve and then of Adam" (Achtemeier, 100–101).

Does Grace Encourage Sin? (6:1–23)

A couple has a terrible disagreement. The split between them is so great, it seems they may never be connected again. Then, in a breakthrough moment, the impass is crossed, and they are reconciled. In the process of breaking up and healing, their bond grows even stronger. This experience may mislead some to conclude that couples should break up because "making up" is so enjoyable.

In chapter 6 Paul speaks to the age-old question of grace and sin: "Should we continue in sin in order grace may abound?" (6:1). The clear answer is "No." He then introduces an insight that is repeated in other letters, specifically Galatians 2:20. To be baptized into Christ, to share faith in God through Christ, is also to share in Christ's death in a very real, though spiritual, way. To die to the power of sin and self is to experience our own "I" crucified by God's love for us. When we share in Christ's death, that is, when the death of Christ

> "Paul was alive to the charge that his gospel of salvation apart from the law encouraged immorality."—Calvin J. Roetzel, *The Letters of Paul*, 4th ed.,109.

humbles us and shames us because we realize that our pride and fear helped kill Christ, we also share in his resurrection (6:3–5). This theme is then repeated and expanded in 6:5–11.

As you study this passage, remember that at times Romans is like a symphony in which one theme is repeated and developed in a variety of ways.

The chapter concludes with a passage that begins, "*Therefore,* do not let sin exercise dominion in your mortal bodies" (6:12–23). Humans will be a slave to something. The question is to what? The Pauline alternative to being a slave to sin is to become, by faith, out of gratitude, a

> "We are members of a new race, whose goal for the first time can be something other than rebellion against God and ensuing death."—Paul J. Achtemeier, *Romans*, Interpretation, 105.

slave to God, which leads to sanctification. Notice that Paul says he is making this human analogy because of our "natural limitations" (6:19). "The wages of sin is death, but the free gift of God is eternal life in Christ Jesus our Lord" (6:23). To trust God is to discover a higher meaning of life; to trust self is to experience the horrors of death.

? Questions for Reflection

1. This unit asserts that faith is often recognized when looking back over one's life and seeing the presence of God. What are ways to recognize the presence of God?

2. Achtemeier says that suffering and disappointment are two realities that, singly or together, are all too familiar in the life of the Christian. They call into question the validity of faith, or at least its redemptive power. "Such questions surface not only in the midst of these experiences but also in times of self-examination when introspection lays bare the weakness of one's faith" (Achtemeier, 92).

Where is one's faith weakest? What role does one's faith play when confronting suffering or doubt?

3. Paul asserts that "one man's act of righteousness leads to justification and life for all" (5:18). Some think that Paul is too permissive in this statement and doesn't emphasize the importance of human response sufficiently. Others suggest Paul is too limiting—that he may be saying that God has decided who will be saved and who won't be saved, or that nothing an individual can do will change God's decree. How does Christ's sacrifice make a difference? What parts do grace and human responsibility play?

4. What do you think Martin Luther meant by the phrase "radical acceptance"?

Beyond Religion to Faith

In the opening verses of chapter 7, Paul enters into a conversation with his readers. The style of verse 1 suggests that Paul wants to make certain his readers are fully engaged with the discussion of faith and law. Romans is not just a letter to read, it is a conversation that involves Paul, the reader, and the Spirit of God.

Paul's opening provides us with an opportunity to stop and ask, What feelings have you developed about Paul's thinking? What in Romans is liberating? What is disturbing? What is confusing? If you had the opportunity to sit down with Paul, what would you ask him? What assumptions in your own faith does Paul challenge with this letter?

Recapping the Main Points

In any study of Paul, it is important to remember the old adage "Some find the theology of Paul appealing, others find the theology of Paul appalling." Different denominations stress different aspects of the redemption/salvation message. Different books in the Bible stress different aspects of God's relationship to creation. The books of the New Testament present Jesus and the church in different ways. Paul's letters, especially Romans, are more "intellectual" than the Gospels.

No one has to like Paul, or even to agree with Paul, but Paul is important to the canon. Across the centuries the church has repeatedly reaffirmed Paul's understanding of Christian faith. The writings of Paul are the largest section of the New Testament. On the other hand, no one book of the Bible is sufficient for our understanding of God. The size and the diversity of Holy Scripture affirm the vastness of God.

As we reflect upon Paul's message to the Romans and debate with Paul's proclamation of the gospel, three observations about Paul will be helpful.

> "Freed from domination by sin and its captive, the law, the Christian can now lead a life led by Spirit, not law."—Paul J. Achtemeier, *Romans*, Interpretation, 115.

1. Paul's own personal experience with the gospel revealed to him how self-centered he had been. Paul wrote Romans out of a powerful firsthand experience of being a Jew seeking to live by the law, judging others, opposing and persecuting the church. After the encounter with God on the Damascus road, Paul's understanding of sin went through a radical reorientation. This reorientation is the foundation of much of what follows in this letter.

Paul understands *sin* as beginning with the desire of Adam and Eve to "be like God, knowing good from evil." To be a child of Adam and Eve is to see this same desire in our own lives. Adam and Eve failed to trust God; therefore, they also failed to obey God. Some essential points in Paul's theology to keep in mind are these:

—Until humans can trust that God is right, they will trust themselves more than they trust God.

—Part of trusting God is living with mystery, including the mystery of the exact specifics of how salvation will work itself out in every human life.

—When people trust the love of God and the promises of God, they need no longer fear life, even with the adverse realities of suffering, nor should they fear death, even with its promise of judgment.

—However much sin may multiply, grace will always multiply much more.

2. Paul's great joy as a Christian is the absolute conviction that the life, death, and resurrection of Jesus have the power (but not yet the reality) of breaking down every barrier to human reconciliation and to human-divine reconciliation. However, for this reconciliation to occur, the gospel has to be proclaimed and it has to create response. For Paul, the initiative for reconciliation begins with God, who chose Abraham and Sarah, who sent Jesus, who creates and sustains the church.

Faith begins with God; faith is sustained by the Spirit of God. The Christian church has developed a variety of ways of understanding how faith occurs. Different ecclesiastical traditions have very different ideas on how faith occurs. The evangelical tradition emphasizes the importance of human response to God's claim upon us. The Roman Catholic tradition stresses the significance of the sacraments as the path to faith. The Orthodox branches of the church affirm the importance of pure doctrine.

Paul is urging us to look beyond all human understanding of faith, to affirm that faith begins with God and that shared faith, rightly presented, creates response. God gets the glory and credit for the response as well as for the initiative, for God created us with the capacity to respond.

3. Paul believes that the victory of God's grace over sin will not be fully evident until "the end of the age," but, by the power of God's spirit, we can perceive the victory now. We find both peace and glory in that perception. This is a bold affirmation, and it is either embraced in whole or not at all. Our rational, pragmatic selves have trouble with the affirmation because it challenges the way we see all of life, and therefore the way we order every aspect of our lives. When we are honest, we know that we do not embrace this radical transformation with our whole self. Such honesty opens us to rejoice in the grace of God, yet the grace of God does not grant us the right to be satisfied with our half-hearted response. Therefore, through faith, by grace, we are being transformed from being slaves to ourselves and joyfully, willingly, become slaves to the righteous will of God, which Paul calls sanctification.

Love and the Law
(7:1–6)

As Paul continues to wrestle with the way the law loses power over us yet still exercises authority for us, he gives a specific example (7:1–3). The law of Moses controls our outward actions during our lifetime; the law of God, instilled in us through faith, exercises authority over our whole being for all eternity (7:4). To "bear the fruit of God" is to live in such a way that we fulfill the will of God, which is prescribed by the law.

The fruit of the Spirit is love, joy, peace . . .

For both Martin Luther and John Calvin, love is a response of faith. The gospel sets us free to love God. We love God by sharing God's love with other people. Love is a *response* of faith, not the *source* or beginning of faith.

The Paradox of the Law (7:7–14)

John Calvin's first use of the law is stated by Paul in verse 7: "If it had not been for the law, I would not have known sin." The law shows us sin. The law can deceive us, by leading us to believe that through obedience to the law we become righteous; therefore, the law is dangerous to our spiritual well-being. However, the law is also necessary, for the law shows us sin.

The distinction between the good and sacred purpose of the law as opposed to the dangerous and evil possibilities of the law is captured in the distinction between *faith* and *religion*. Religion is the human attempt to define a way to be righteous. Believing that subscribing to certain doctrines will guarantee salvation is a form of religion. Believing that performing certain rituals, or participating in Bible study, or avid church attendance will lead to salvation is religion. Believing that saying certain words, such "I accept Jesus Christ as my Lord and Savior" will guarantee our right relationship with God is religion. *Faith,* on the other hand, is trusting God, seeking to obey God while recognizing that our attempts at obedience are always inadequate. Faith is confidence in God's love and God's grace, realizing we never deserve that grace, nor do we fully understand to whom grace is given or to whom mercy is shown, but nevertheless trusting that God will do what is right for all people.

Religion is the human attempt to honor God. Though often noble in the attempt, it usually leads to failure, sin, and guilt. Faith is a gift from God that brings honor and dignity to human life. Faith creates hope and righteousness.

The Human Predicament and God's Power to Transform (7:8–25)

Paul uses the image of death and life in a symbolic way in verses 8–13. Then Paul eloquently describes the human predicament in verses

14–24. The response of faith is given in 7:25. Note that the first response is confession and an expression of hopelessness: "Wretched man that I am! Who will rescue me from this body of death?" (7:24).

The second response is affirmation and thanksgiving: "Thanks be to God through Jesus Christ our Lord!" (7:25). The third response is transformation of thinking: "With my mind I am a slave to the law of God, but with my flesh I am a slave to the law of sin" (7:26).

> "The problem is not with the will, the problem is the inability to do what one knows to be good and therefore wants to do because one is no longer under one's own control." Paul J. Achtemeier, *Romans*, Interpretation, 122.

The use of the word "mind" in 7:25 speaks of the power of God's grace to transform the way we think. The statement that follows is recognition that just because we begin to think a new way and to believe in a new way, our actions are not always obedient. Thus Reinhold Niebuhr's truth, "Sin persists, even among the redeemed" (see Niebuhr, *The Nature and Destiny of Man*, vol. 1, 178–207).

> "Here Paul is giving us his own spiritual autobiography and laying bare his very heart and soul."—William Barclay, *The Letter to the Romans*, Daily Study Bible, 94.

C. K. Barrett says that this passage is often taken as the story of Paul's conversion but that something deeper than a conversion story is communicated here. The great affirmation of this chapter is Paul's continual dependence upon Christ. The practice of a religion cannot save a person; salvation comes from God through Christ, not just at one time in our life, but for all eternity (Barrett, 37).

Spirit and Flesh (8:1–11)

Romans 8 opens with the magnificent words, "There is therefore now no condemnation for those who are in Christ Jesus." The coming of Christ frees us from self-inflicted condemnation (cf. John 3:17). "The Spirit of life" now rules all of creation. "The Spirit of him who raised Jesus from the dead" gives life to us also (8:11). Barrett points out that the opening verses of chapter 8 point back to the opening verses of chapter 7 (Barrett, 38). The terms "spirit" and "flesh" do not refer to two parts of human nature but, rather, to two ways of living. The way of the flesh is self-centered rebellion and idolatry; it is not the way of the body or the individual as much as it is an orientation to the ways of the world. The way of the Spirit is life in bondage to the Creator, in which Christ is freely acknowledged as Lord (Achtemeier, 131–34).

An example of flesh versus spirit would be our current discomfort with the status of college athletics and, to some extent, professional athletics. In many major sports, the "spirit" of college athletics has been lost; the worldly perspective has gained control. We who love college athletics find ourselves increasingly uncomfortable with the values some major sports instill, not just in athletes, but in children, youth, adults, as well as in society in general.

A second example would be the way our lives have become "entertainment driven" as opposed to family, service, or faith centered. Neil Postman's critique on society, *Amusing Ourselves to Death*, communicates some Pauline concepts. Postman suggests that our obsession with leisure, recreation, and entertainment may ultimately bring more harm to the social order, be more out of order with God's will for creation, than overtly illegal acts. Entertainment and recreation appear to be "good"; illegal acts are known to be "bad."

"Christian freedom, Paul insists, is freedom to serve God."—Stephen Westerholm in Richard Longnecker, *The Road From Damascus: The Impact of Paul's Conversion on His Life, Thought, and Ministry* (Grand Rapids: Wm. B. Eerdmans Publishing Co., 1997), 162.

A third example is our tendency to push ourselves to do good things, even sacred things, beyond our capacity—or the capacity of others—to enjoy or grow through the experience. As a wise friend once said, "The most important decisions in life (and in ministry) may be deciding which worthwhile things *not* to do, and then finding the courage *not* to do them." The way of the flesh is to cram as much fun, education, service, or whatever else we think is good and right into our lives as possible. Reinhold Niebuhr insisted that the chief manifestation of sin in our time is our failure to recognize that we are finite, limited in time, energy, intelligence, and resources. This failure leads to a unique "works righteousness" in which we imagine that our life, or our community, or our world will be better if we just "do" one more good thing or achieve one more worthwhile goal. We become self-deceived, thinking that the more good things we do for ourselves or for others, the more fulfilled (righteous) we will be, and the less guilt we have. However, at some point in our

"Wanting reward from God for our goodness betrays an attitude that opens the door once more for the power of sin to enter our lives."—Paul J. Achtemeier, *Romans*, Interpretation, 125.

lives, the more we try to do, the less dependent we become on the grace of God.

The way of the Spirit will lead us to do good, but it will also empower us to enjoy life and people, and to enjoy God. Remember that the very first question in the Westminster Shorter Catechism addresses this question about the source of life's meaning when it affirms that the chief end of human life is to glorify God and to enjoy God forever (Question 1, paraphrased). The way of the Spirit will lead us to do good; the Spirit will also empower us to enjoy life and people, and to enjoy God.

Reflections on Romans at the Midpoint

As we approach the heart of this letter, perhaps it is a good time to stop, reflect on the message to this point, and acknowledge that the language in Romans continues to be a challenge. Words such as *righteousness* (doing what is right and good for all of creation), *justification* (being made "right," through love and forgiveness), and *sanctification* (becoming "righteous" in response to the love of God and the indwelling power of the Holy Spirit) are not part of our normal vocabulary. More familiar words such as *reconciliation* (moving beyond guilt and loneliness through the love and forgiveness of God), *sin* (pride, self-interest, denial of finiteness versus evil or immoral actions) and *salvation* (joyful trust and obedience toward God) receive a new or different meaning through Romans.

This emphasis on vocabulary reminds us that Romans is not history or narrative. It is not even a "letter" in the usual sense of that word. Romans is early Christian theology; it is "faith seeking understanding." Romans is Paul's desire, led by the Holy Spirit, to explain and to affirm what has happened in human lives and in the whole of creation, through the life, death, and resurrection of Christ and the establishment of the church.

Throughout Romans, Paul is seeking both to understand and to affirm what has changed in his life and in all of creation through the life, death, and resurrection of Jesus Christ. Major themes for Paul are:

> ### Want to Know More?
>
> **About the concept of bearing fruit in the Bible?** See Leland Ryken et al., *Dictionary of Biblical Imagery* (Downers Grove, Ill.: InterVarsity Press, 1998), 310–11.
>
> **About spirit and flesh?** See Paul J. Achtemeier, *Romans*, Interpretation, 131–37; Alasdair I. C. Heron, *The Holy Spirit* (Philadelphia: Westminster Press, 1983), 44–60.

1. The law loses power over us, yet still exercises authority for us.
2. Reliance upon the law increases our desire to be like God, deceiving us into thinking we know good from evil.
3. The law leads to sin and guilt. Faith creates hope and righteousness.
4. The gospel will lead us to do good, but it will also empower us to enjoy life and people, and to enjoy God.

? Questions for Reflection

1. This unit has intentionally gone back and summarized the content and themes of Romans up to this point. What are the key tenets of the Christian faith? How would you explain them to someone else?
2. Think about your own image of a good and fulfilled life. How does this image compare with Paul's description of "life in the Spirit" in the opening verses of chapter 8?
3. What is Paul's understanding of the relationship between the resurrection of Jesus and salvation?
4. How do the words *grace* and *peace* take on new meaning in this unit?

The "Convictions" of Our Faith

Different scholars outline Romans in different ways. One respected way of dividing the letter suggests that the passage for this lesson concludes the second major section of the letter. This approach to outlining Romans identifies the first four chapters as a major section, the next four chapters are the second division, and then the last seven chapters are the third major component. In Romans 8, Paul turns from struggling with the law and servitude to sin, toward that which saves the Christian from law and sin and represents the promise of God's final victory over sin. Romans 8 is one of the great passages of scripture, both because of its affirmations of God's power and its insight into the struggles of the Christian's life.

In the last chapter we looked at the way the confessional statements in Romans 7:14–25 lead into the first verse of Romans 8, giving us another Pauline *therefore*. When we see ourselves as sinners who have been crucified with Christ, yet we live, there is therefore no condemnation for us because we know that we have died to sin. When we lament the good we cannot do and the evil we persist in doing and cry out, "Who will rescue me from this body of death?" we come to know that there is no condemnation for those who see Christ as the proof of God's amazing love for us (Romans 5:8).

Transformation (8:12–13)

Based on this powerful personal and confessional experience, Paul says, "So then, brothers and sisters, we are debtors" (8:12). We are debtors, not to flesh and blood, but to the Spirit. The "Spirit of God"

51

is that transformation of the way we see ourselves, see others, and see God which comes through confession, repentance, and the assurance of pardon which is the essence of Christian salvation. It is not "our faith" that gives new life to our bodies; it is the "Spirit of God."

> "The transformation wrought by God's Spirit is such that one becomes a foreigner to the culture to which one once belonged."—Paul J. Achtemeier, *Romans*, Interpretation, 140.

As we read through this familiar portion of Romans, note the continued "theocentric" nature of Paul's writings. The distinction Paul makes between "Spirit" and "flesh" is the difference between an "autonomous" way of life and a "theonomous" way of life, which we discussed in Unit 4 of this book. To be rescued (saved) by God is to be set free from trusting oneself, or from trusting our ability to obey the law, and to have a passionate desire to follow God's will.

C. K. Barrett says that the theological movement that occurs is one away from "Out of self concern, I owe it to myself to do thus and so" to "Out of gratitude, I owe it to God to do thus and so" (8:12–13; Barrett, 42).

Children of God (8:14–17)

The affirmation of the preceding verses then leads to the great words of 8:14: "All who are led by the Spirit of God are children of God." Another way of stating this phrase would be, "We who have come to

"We are children of God."

see the futility of trusting our own desires no longer seek to obey the law. Rather, we now put our trust in the will of God, through the power of the Spirit of God, which is the Spirit of love and grace. This inner transformation marks us as 'children of God.'"

We no longer are controlled by fear; we now are controlled by love, a love that comes not through our deserving but through our "adoption." Paul proceeds to introduce an image from his experience with Roman adoption law, a rather complex procedure his readers would have known.

An adopted child is a *chosen* child. An adopted child lays aside the debts and obligations of the previous family; the old life no longer has any claim. The adopted child becomes a new person, with a new life, heir to the father's estate. Using this image, Paul says, that when we cry out to God, "Abba" (Daddy!), the very word is an extension of the Spirit of God, enabling our spirit to know that we are children

> "God through the Spirit not only treats us 'just like family,' but actually unites us into [God's] family."—Paul J. Achtemeier, *Romans,* Interpretation, 137.

of God. If we are children of God, then we are heirs of God and joint heirs with Christ.

This status as a child of God will call us to suffer as Christ suffered. Paul does not deny the reality of suffering in the lives of Christian people, nor does he attribute suffering to the intentional will of God. He interprets suffering as a family event. When we are part of the family of God, we suffer, but we also share the assurance of being glorified, as Christ is glorified (8:15–17). Achtemeier suggests that this passage has the power to redefine our understanding of family (Achtemeier, 140ff.). To understand "family" from a Christian perspective is to understand the power of suffering. The strongest family is not necessarily the one that has the most fun together. The family that suffers together for the well-being of a particular family member or for the well-being of the larger community may have an even stronger sense of identity, one that can also be understood as glory.

Paul is clear that suffering is part of the human condition. Suffering leads to a maturity of life and faith that would not otherwise be present. This conviction is part of the "stumbling block" of the gospel. The understanding of suffering present in the letter to the Romans and in Christianity is one of the enduring concepts that gives a new shape to the meaning of life. An attempt for people of faith to understanding suffering and the will of God is called *theodicy. Theodicy* has always perplexed the Judeo-Christian tradition. Theodicy is the desire to understand why a good and loving God allows suffering, especially of the innocent. In Romans 5 and 8, Paul directly addresses this issue. He speaks of suffering as part of God's plan to bring creation to maturity. God does not always inflict suffering upon people; rather, suffering is often the result of sin. Therefore, it is part of having limited freedom. Suffering can be an arena in which God's love and God's power is known, rather than God's direct wrath. The power of God to transform suffering into good is symbolized in the crucifixion and resurrection. The resurrection therefore becomes a sign pointing us to God's ability to transform all of creation into the kingdom of God. Suffering remains a mystery, but it is also an area of life in which the direct presence of God can be known.

Living in Hope (8:18–25a)

Using slightly different language, Paul then returns to a familiar theme, the troubled state of contemporary life. "The sufferings of the present time are not worth comparing with the glory that shall be revealed to us." Living in hope means we live with confidence that nothing lies beyond the scope of God's loving purpose and power. We can endure current suffering, even injustice and oppression, because we are confident that God will "do right" by creation.

Paul's vision involves far more than any individual human being. Humanity sinned voluntarily; all of nature became involved in the consequences (8:20). Paul proceeds to lay out a hope that encompasses the whole created order. "Creation waits with eager longing for the revealing of the children of God. . . . We know that the whole creation has been groaning in labor pains until now; and not only the creation, but we ourselves, who have the first fruits of the Spirit, [we also] groan inwardly while we wait for adoption, the redemption of our bodies." This waiting also involves hope. "In hope we were saved" (8:19–25).

Want to Know More?

About the concept of adoption in the Bible? See Leland Ryken et al., *Dictionary of Biblical Imagery* (Downers Grove, Ill.: InterVarsity Press, 1998), 14–15.

About eschatology? See Donald K. McKim, *Theological Turning Points: Major Issues in Christian Thought* (Atlanta: John Knox Press, 1988), 151–65. For a thorough discussion about New Testament references to the end times, see William Barclay, *At the Last Trumpet: Jesus Christ and the End of Time* (Louisville, Ky.: Westminster John Knox Press, 1998).

The emphasis in Romans on all of creation as opposed to an emphasis on individuals leads to *eschatology*. Eschatology, literally, "the word about the end" (*eschaton*), speaks of how God will deal with the whole created order. The book of Revelation is eschatological, but so, too, is Jesus' teaching about the kingdom of God or the kingdom of heaven. Traditional theology has always insisted that God is concerned about individuals and about the whole of creation. Creation is the arena within which God is revealed. Creation began with God; creation will end with God. Romans affirms that creation will lead to the victorious love of God.

How humans live together becomes a sign of God's future rule. Therefore, Romans is concerned about government, as we will see in chapter 9. Government is the art, science, and theology of living together in creation as community, under both divine and human authority.

This passage has several helpful parallels elsewhere in the Bible. Note the imagery of labor pains and new birth and the parallel with the story of Nicodemus in John 3. Also, this passage tells of the reversal of the curse upon the earth in Genesis 3. The concept that hope rises out of faith relates to the Abraham story. First comes faith, the trust in God's righteousness that is ours through Jesus. Then comes hope, the conviction we cannot prove, but believe, that God will "do right" by all of creation, keeping the promise first made to Abraham and Sarah.

Good News (Romans 8:25b–30)

Now we come to the great insight and promise of Romans. "We wait for [the fulfillment of creation] with patience" (8:25b). But this hope and this waiting do not come easily. "The Spirit helps us in our weakness." "We do not know how to pray as we ought." "That very Spirit intercedes for us with sighs too deep for words." "God . . . knows what is the mind of the Spirit, because the Spirit intercedes for the saints [those who have faith] according to the will of God" (8:26–28).

The intercession of the Spirit then allows *us* (the saints) to "know that all things work together for good for those who love God, who are called according to his purpose" (8:28). C. H. Dodd is helpful in his commentary as he points out that this text is not suggesting that the universe is an orderly system in which everything will work out all right in the end. This is not Paul's attitude, nor is it the approach of the New Testament. The world does not have an inherent tendency to get better and better. The redemption of humanity and the redemption of creation is an act of sheer grace, free and unconditioned, which comes from God alone. The hope that is ours as Christians is not embedded in the created order; it is a hope that is due solely to an act of God in history (Dodd, 137–38).

> "Creation is standing at the window, looking out in keen anticipation for the redemption of the children of God, for just as it was our sin that brought creation into subjection to decay and death, it is our redemption that shall bring life. And creation will look out the window and one day will see the pageantry of Eden again"—Fred Craddock, "What We Do Not Know," *Journal for Preachers*, Advent 1998, 34.

The convictions in this passage lead to an important secondary statement about predestination. Predestination rises out of the conviction that God will "do right" by creation and that Jesus' death and resurrection reverses the curse upon all of creation brought on by the sin of Adam and Eve. Predestination rises out of hope, which overrules fear of judgment. Karl Barth insists that "The Love of God is not a 'property,' which [humans] may achieve or inherit, or which inheres in them. Rightly understood, there are not Christians; there is only the eternal opportunity of becoming Christian—an opportunity at once accessible and inaccessible to all [people] (Barth, 321).

> "The Holy Spirit is the gift by which we know God in part, and we know that we are already fully known. The Holy Spirit is God's promise that one day we will also fully know."—David L. Bartlett, *Romans,* Westminster Bible Companion, 74.

Achtemeier points out three specific proclamations of good news in this passage: (1) There is the assurance that the result of Adam's rebellion will be set right by God in the final transformation of reality. (2) God has restored rightful communication between God and human beings, through Spirit-directed prayer. (3) Our destiny is no longer in our own hands, but in the hands of an all-powerful and all-loving God, whose purpose is redemption (Achtemeier, 142–44).

Conclusion (8:31–39)

The convictions of the preceding passage then lead to a majestic conclusion. Paul recognizes that many things in life appear to contradict the affirmations he has just made. The sufferings of this present age are real, but in the death of Christ, the conviction that God is for us is also made real. If Christ died for us, then what in the world can make us doubt God's love for us? Paul lists many of the "things" that appear to have a power to separate us from God; then he affirms that neither these "things," nor "anything else in all of creation, will be able to separate us from the love of God in Christ Jesus our Lord" (8:39b).

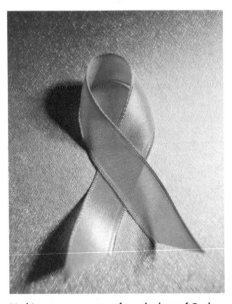

Nothing can separate us from the love of God.

Like a strip of tangled duct tape that cannot be pulled apart, such is the binding love of God in Christ Jesus. In an exhaustive inventory, Paul names anything and everything, only to conclude that nothing can separate us from God's love. Nothing.

The gift of believing this promise, of trusting in this relationship, is the Pauline understanding of "salvation." Calvin's *Commentary on Romans* further develops understanding of salvation, as does the third book of Calvin's *Institutes of the Christian Religion.* Unlike Luther, Calvin is more concerned with discerning the meaning and purpose of human life than with escaping from deep internal guilt. Reflecting on Paul's words, Calvin writes, "God does not ascribe our faults and corruption to us, but receives us as his children. It is necessary that we be pure, but this is an imputed purity in as much as we borrow it from Jesus Christ. There is also an actual purity, or as it is said, the goodness of God which works in us. This shows itself by its effects, for God renews us by his Holy Spirit and corrects our evil affection. In short, he lives in us and rules in us" (Calvin, *Commentary on Romans*, 359–60).

? Questions for Reflection

1. When you think of freedom, what concepts and images come to your mind? When Paul teaches about freedom, what is his vision for this word?
2. Some believe that misfortune is a reflection of God's judgment. What do these verses say to that belief? What is the cause of misfortune?
3. If you were to write a paraphrase of Romans 8:31–39, what extremes from the twenty-first century would you list?
4. The word "Spirit" occurs at least twenty times in this passage. What are the works of the Spirit according to Paul?

8 Romans 9:1–11:26

The Promises of God to Israel and to Us

This chapter examines the third major section of Paul's letter. In the first section, chapters 1–4, Paul affirms God's rule over all of creation. Using the twin themes of grace and wrath, Paul introduces us to the problems that have plagued the created order from the beginning. He also makes specific reference to the promise of God given to the Jews.

In the second major section, chapters 5–8, Paul shifts to the challenge of the gospel and the ways in which God's revelation in Christ confirms the law at the same time it overthrows the power of the law. In the third major section, which is the portion of Romans covered by this chapter, Paul addresses the issue of God's commitment to Israel, which Achtemeier calls "God's Lordship and the Problem of the Future: Israel and God's Gracious Plan" (Achtemeier, x). For Paul, a major questions looms: How do we understand the covenant God made with the Jews in light of the covenant God has now made with the church? If the Jews were already God's chosen people, how could God now choose the Gentiles? The very nature of God, the attributes of God that cause God to be God, are at the heart of this section as Paul wrestles with an understanding of God that keeps God faithful to God's own promises.

What of God's promises to the Jews?

What about the Jews? (Romans 9)

Notice the significant shift in tone of voice and attitude at the beginning of the chapter. Until now, Paul has been making bold affirmations about the power of the gospel and the power of God. But God has made certain promises to the Jews. Many Jews have not believed the gospel. What do we say about persistent unbelief in the lives of God's own chosen and loved children? How can God's plan and promise for the redemption of all of creation be complete without the Jews (Achtemeier, 153)? This question, of course, is not just about Paul's struggle to understand the relationship of the Jews to God; the question speaks directly to any doctrine of salvation. How can anyone be happy about salvation unless everyone is happy?

After expressing deep grief and confusion, but not anger (9:1–5), that his own people have been unreceptive to the gospel of Christ, Paul utilizes Old Testament characters (9:1–6) to demonstrate that God's word has not failed. His examples—Abraham, Isaac, Rebecca, Jacob, and Esau, Moses, and Pharaoh—are not all logical ones. For instance, Paul does not refer to the promise God made to Hagar and to Ishmael (Genesis 21). Paul does, however, stress the freedom God exercises in showing mercy to those whom God chooses, people who are often unfaithful and undeserving. To be chosen by God is to be a recipient of God's grace. To be numbered among the chosen is not a matter of parentage or biology. No one can claim that God owes mercy (9:11–12, 16). Mercy is always a gift, which leads to faith; mercy is not inherited nor is it determined by faith or works (9:13–15, 18).

In verse 19, Paul enters a dialogical debate. Paul's point is hard but true: human beings deserve the wrath of God; mercy is always an undeserved gift. Therefore, those who receive wrath are getting what they deserve, and those who receive mercy are getting better than they deserve (9:25, 29).

Achtemeier says that Paul is speaking here of *predestination,* not *predeterminism* or "fatalism." Predestination speaks of God's foreordaining the final outcome of all. Predeterminism is the conviction that every event is already "predetermined," eliminating choice or "free will." As with a journey, predestination holds that God knows the journey's end, but predeterminism holds that God controls every turn or stop along the way.

The Bible, in both the Old Testament and the New, tells repeatedly of people who have been called by God, yet who fail to be faithful to God. God's people fail to obey, they fail to understand, and they fail to trust, yet God acts with mercy toward them. God's power is such that no failure, however desperate, can thwart God's redemptive plan (Achtemeier, 157–58). No human action can override the sovereignty of God.

> "Even though you intended to do harm to me, God intended it for good" (Gen. 51:20).

This is a radical and complex proposal; however, it speaks to the heart of Paul's theology in Romans. God, who has been gracious, can be trusted to continue to be gracious, even to the Jews. God is not bound by genetics or by promises to be faithful to all Jews. The grace God showed in choosing the Jews is again evident in the call to faith that occurs in Christ. The call of God originates in grace; the call is sustained by grace. The grace of God is the attribute that makes God righteous.

Achtemeier is adamant that a careful reading of Romans 9 reveals that Paul's affirmation in this chapter is about God's attitude toward Israel and not about the way God determines the fate of individuals—in Paul's time or in our time. These verses do not support views of predeterminism. This passage reveals the ways God's grace is big enough to include the Gentiles. Further, Achtemeier also insists that this chapter makes clear that Christians cannot be anti-Semitic, for Jews are saved by God's grace, just as are Christians and Gentiles (Achtemeier, 165).

This chapter in Romans is important for establishing the authority of the Old Testament in the life of the early church. Paul insists that there is continuity and consistency between the God of the Old Testament and the Father of Jesus Christ. Using the metaphor of the olive tree which occurs in a later passage (11:17–21), Paul is saying, "These roots support you."

Salvation Is for All (Romans 10)

In chapter 10, Paul continues exploring the question raised in 9:30, "What then are we to say?" Note that Paul has used this question five times now, each time to indicate that he is wrestling with a difficult issue.

Paul loves the Jewish people, and he is convinced that God loves them also. The language in chapter 10 reflects anguish, confusion, and conviction. This language embodies the Christian attitude toward those who are "outside the gospel." The passage even includes the tragic possibility that religious people may reject God because they have become too religious—believing that by their human response to God's initiative they have become equal to God in the salvation process. They have misunderstood that they are but children of God, recipients of God's saving grace.

Paul's point is that *both* the law and Jesus lead us to trust God, a trust that is lived out through confessing Jesus to be Lord and believing that God raised Jesus from the dead. Note that the command to "call upon the name of the Lord" is a quote from the Old Testament prophet Joel. This chapter in Romans is important in establishing the authority of the Old Testament for the early church. Again, the emphasis is not so much on believing in Jesus as on believing in and trusting the God whom Jesus fully reveals as righteous and powerful.

This chapter stresses the importance of proclamation and responsible listening but concludes with a reminder of God's grace. In verses 9–10 Paul appears to be saying that words alone are not sufficient for salvation. But salvation is more than a verbal formula; it involves a relationship with God based upon trust in God.

> **Want to Know More?**
>
> **About predestination?** See Shirley C. Guthrie, *Christian Doctrine*, rev. ed. (Louisville, Ky.: Westminster John Knox Press, 1994), 118–41.
>
> **About God's sovereignty?** See Daniel L. Migliore, *The Power of God*, Library of Living Faith (Philadelphia: Westminster Press, 1983), 15–74. For an academic discussion about limits to God's power, see E. Frank Tupper, *A Scandalous Providence: The Jesus Story of the Compassion of God* (Macon, Ga.: Mercer University Press, 1995), 326–31, 358–61.

> "If the only way one can learn how to respond appropriately to God's grace is listening, one had better listen carefully!"—Paul J. Achtemeier, *Romans*, Interpretation, 175.

The Error of Figuring It Out

The teachings of the letter to the Romans such as those in this chapter have caused Romans to become the basis of what is called "neo-orthodoxy." Neo-orthodoxy is an understanding of Christian faith that has deep respect for traditional, orthodox doctrines of Christianity, combined with a respect for science and technology. Revelation and inspiration are honored; the Word of God is authoritative, but the capacity of the human mind to critique, reflect, and synthesize is also respected.

The Roman model of faith affirms the traditional teachings of faith, including the sacredness of the Old Testament and the covenant with Israel. At the same time, Paul affirms the Christian faith in a carefully reasoned way, much aware of the challenges and questions of his day.

In a sermon on Romans 10:1–13, the great twentieth-century theologian Reinhold Niebuhr said:

> The words, "I bear them witness that they have a zeal of God but not according to knowledge," were spoken by St. Paul to his own people and generation. They nevertheless have a remarkable applicability to the humanistic age that began in the eighteenth century and is now drawing to a close in such sorry anarchy of international and social wars. . . . The modern age substituted the God of reason and nature for the God of revealed religion. (Niebuhr, *Beyond Tragedy*, 229)

Niebuhr is echoing Paul, as both insist that any age that thinks it has "figured out" how to understand God, or how to achieve salvation, has fallen into the trap of zeal without knowledge.

The Irrevocable Gifts and Calling of God (Romans 11)

Paul pushes forward; he develops the position that even the unbelief of the Jews occurs within God's gracious purposes because this unbelief provides the way for a mission to the Gentiles.

The chapter opens with a statement on God's power to preserve a faithful remnant. The covenant does not depend upon people; it depends upon God's grace (11:5). Gentiles are now included among God's chosen people, but not to the exclusion of the Jews (11:11–12). If God, in sending Jesus, has caused the Jews to be unfaithful to God, then Gentiles should be grateful for the grace of God that now includes them. However, their rejection of Jesus does not mean that God's grace has been withdrawn from the Jews.

Paul's position in verses 25–36 is complicated, but it is the heart of the Pauline understanding of grace and of salvation. In a way that Paul cannot fully explain, the stumbling of the Jews becomes a means of salvation for the Gentiles, and vice versa (11:30). Unbelieving Jews are still

God's people (11:1–2). Paul remains confident of their salvation and looks forward to a time when Old Testament people and New Testament people will be one in Christ (11:26).

Paul also loves the Gentiles. He rejoices in their faith, but Paul wants to make certain that the Gentiles do not take pride in their faith. Paul refers to them as a wild olive shoot grafted onto the cultivated olive tree, a familiar picture of historic Israel (11:7ff.). With this vivid imagery, Paul warns them and us, "Do not become proud, but stand in awe" (11:20).

> "The irony and tragedy is that while Gentiles who never sought that righteousness are now attaining it, Israel as a whole has failed to reach it despite earnest effort to that end."—James D. G. Dunn, *Romans 9–16*, Word Biblical Commentary, vol. 38B (Dallas, Tex.: Word Books, 1988), 592.

Complicated though this passage is, Paul's words reveal the heart of his understanding of the inclusive nature of God's grace and faithfulness. Paul has confidence in the fulfillment of God's purposes for humankind. As Paul concludes this affirmation of God's faithfulness and conviction that God does not revoke an earlier call, Paul makes a bold statement. He suggests that human imprisonment to sin through disobedience is part of a plan for all human beings to experience God's mercy.

This chapter and this section end with words of confession and adoration. It is as though, after trying to be logical, Paul bursts into song, realizing that words alone cannot express the mystery of grace or of salvation—"The gifts and calling of God are irrevocable!"

God Is Working God's Purpose Out

The pages of these chapters reverberate with power. The church's passion to share the gospel derives from a gospel that transforms life from fear and lawlessness toward gratitude and obedience.

The need for evangelism is not minimized by the assurances of grace. However, the church need not be frantic. God is in control; God is gracious. God is working God's purpose out in creation. We are part of that purpose, but the purpose does not depend upon us. The fulfillment of God's purpose is dependent upon God's graciousness.

> "Part of the good news of the gospel is that we are in fact not gods and that therefore the future does not lie in our manifestly incapable hands."—Paul J. Achtemeier, *Romans*, Interpretation, 161–62.

The need for evangelism is not minimized by grace, but the inclination to be judgmental is soundly condemned. Paul's message is a much-needed restraint upon our frenzied, task-driven expressions of evangelism and church programs. The lines of the old mission hymn capture Paul's convictions:

> God is working His purpose out . . .
> By the mouth of many messengers goes forth the voice of God . . .
> All we can do is nothing worth, unless God blesses the deed . . .

> Yet, nearer and nearer draws the time,
> The time that shall surely be,
> When the earth shall be filled with the glory of God,
> As the waters cover the sea.

> (Arthur Campbell Ainger)

? Questions for Reflection

1. What guidance do these chapters provide for appropriate Christian-Jewish relationships today? How do the events of the Holocaust inform our reading of Romans and our relationship with Jews? What subtle kinds of anti-Semitism are present around you?

2. How do you react to Paul's assertion that he would be willing to be "accursed and cut off from Christ for the sake of his people" (9:3)? In some traditions, prospective ministers are asked, "Are you willing to be damned for the sake of the gospel and glory of God?" How would these two statements affect individuals seeking or accepting positions of leadership?

3. Paul shares great anguish as he asks the question, "How can God's plan and promise for the redemption of all creation be complete without the Jews?" Paul is advocating an inclusive understanding of God's grace. What might be your response to the possibility that God's grace and mercy may be so deep and so wide as to include individuals who don't meet our standards? What if those individuals included the likes of Judas or Hitler?

4. The twists and turns of life present some ironic occurrences. What was intended for good sometimes sours, and sometimes a bad event has positive consequences. What are some examples of things that have turned out better than intended?

After Talking the Talk, How Do We Walk the Walk?

Having proclaimed the power of the gospel and emphasized the undeserved mercy of God, Paul begins to give instructions on the Christian life. He speaks practically about ethical issues that first-century Christians faced, and that future Christians would also confront.

Notice the oft-recurring Pauline *therefore* in 12:1. The instructions in this portion of Romans rest upon the preceding teachings. Because of God's mercy, we should live to the glory of God by offering our bodies, our very selves, the "embodiment" of our identity, as spiritual worship to God. Those readers of Jewish background would associate the worship of God with animal sacrifice in the temple. Paul now redefines sacrifice for Christians as putting one's very self at God's disposal.

The opening verses of chapter 12 describe the *sanctified* life. The word *perfect* is translated from a Greek word that means "mature, complete," rather than "without blemish." Notice that the transformation Paul seeks comes through the mind first, so that we discern the will of God. As we discern the will of God, gratitude for the mercy of God and trust in the righteousness of

"Present your bodies as a living sacrifice."

God will create a desire to obey God's will. Ethical admonitions are a further sign of the grace of God (Achtemeier, 194).

The opening verses of chapter 12 are among the most beloved words Paul wrote. They have been of inspiration to countless Christians across the ages. They extend the challenge to live, not in conformity to the demands and desires of the world, but in obedience to the will of God. None of us is able to fulfill this vision out of our own resources; the mercies of God both inspire us to seek this vision and equip us to live toward the vision. A key word in this passage is *discern*. We do not "know" the will of God. God's will is discerned, in part through revelation that occurs through God's initiative, and in part through an openness on our part, as we are aware of our own weakness and our own inability to know what is good and right by ourselves. Part of the power of Romans is in Paul's understanding of human personality. The gospel speaks of our own sense of inadequacy. Instead of condemning us and leaving us hopeless, the gospel calls us to a higher way of life, a way of life that becomes a form of spiritual worship.

> "Real worship is not the offering to God of a liturgy, however noble, and a ritual, however magnificient. *Real worship is the offering of everyday life to* [God], not something transacted in a church, but something which sees the whole world as the temple of the living God."—William Barclay, *The Letter to the Romans,* Daily Study Bible, 157.

Embodying the Grace of God (12:3–21)

When we discern the will of God, we are drawn into the church. The church is those *saints* who have heard the gospel and who, "by the mercies of God," have responded, seeking not to "be conformed to this world, but to be transformed by the renewing of their minds." Verses 3–8 describe the Pauline understanding of the church. The description is meant as an illustration of the church rather than as a precise description of attributes that define the church. Verses 9–21 are a list of those personality traits that become outward signs of inward faith. The list could be compared to the gifts of the spirit in Galatians 5:22–23. A Christian does not seek to "do" these things; rather, a Christian is becoming this type of a person. These verses paint a portrait of a Christlike person rather than giving a checklist of desirable behavior.

The goal of the sanctified life is to live in such a way that we prepare ourselves for full citizenship in the kingdom of God (Achtemeier, 196). Christians do not so much seek the reward of heaven as we seek to prepare ourselves for life under God's rule. Our goal is not personal reward; the goal of Christians is to share in the glory of God that will occur when God's will for all of creation is fulfilled. Note that the reference to "saints" in verse 13 refers to the church in Rome and throughout the world (see Romans 1:7).

In verses 14–21, Paul addresses the specific challenge of living in a larger community in which not all are Christian, and some may even persecute the church, as Paul himself had done. Verses 16–18 are particularly important for a life that embodies the grace of God. Notice that Paul does not advocate withdrawing from the larger world but, rather, living in the world in such a way that our life is a witness to the grace of God and power of the gospel. Christianity is an "in the world" faith; disciples of Jesus are called to embody the presence of God amid the pressures and conflicts of life. Discipleship is not a monastic existence.

Romans 12:20 is certain to raise some questions. What do we make of the puzzling line "If your enemies are hungry, feed them; if they are thirsty, give them something to drink; for by doing this way you will heap burning coals on their heads"? The verse is a direct reference to Proverbs 25:21–22, which reads "If your enemies are hungry, give them bread to eat; and if they are thirsty, give them water to drink; for you will heap coals of fire on their heads, and the Lord will reward you." Achtemeier says that "the Christian task is to embody that grace to enemies which is the way of reconciliation and peace. . . . (Paul) is not giving advice on a better way to get back at one's enemies! Rather such treatment is intended to get the enemy to turn away from enmity to friendship. Gracious deeds thus burn away the hate within. . . . That is the way God dealt with us when we were his enemies" (Achtemeier, 202). Paul is clear that if our love is patterned on God's love, we will care for our enemies as well as friends.

> "We know God loves us not because of the way [God] *feels* about us but because of what [God] has *done* for us."—Paul J. Achtemeier, *Romans*, Interpretation, 209.

A popular best-seller by Kathryn Watterson, *Not by the Sword* (New York: Simon & Schuster, 1995), relates the story of a Jewish cantor who chooses to love a Klansman. By initiating a relationship and confronting the Klansman's hate with compassion, the two miraculously become friends.

Duty toward Government Authorities (Romans 13)

Chapter 13 continues the description of the Christian life but does so within the context of obedience to governing authorities. Two points need to be made at the outset of the discussion of this chapter. First, Paul is speaking to a specific historical context: life as a Roman citizen. Paul is proud of his Roman citizenship. The Roman Empire was honored in Jewish teaching; persecution of the Jews by the Romans came later. Second, Paul has keen insight into the need for political order in a fallen world. C. K. Barrett, an Englishman, wrote in 1963: "The state has a claim, not merely on the respect but on the support of Christians. Paul does not contemplate a situation in which there was any prospect of Christians actually taking a personal share in the work of government. (Christians were numerically insignificant in the first century.) . . . Neither irresponsibility nor disrespect is a Christian virtue; and if there are times when conscience compels a Christian to dissent from the social framework, this is in order that political life may be brought more completely into obedience to God" (Barrett, 70).

Life in community requires structure and respect toward those in authority; it also requires taxes. One of Paul's major points in Romans is that Christian faith does not release us from the standards set by law, both God's law and civil law. Note how Paul's understanding of Christianity leaves no room for rabid individualism. The life of Christian faith is lived out in relationships, both vertically with God and horizontally with other people.

"The Christian's freedom from law therefore does not mean freedom from civil law. The believer is just as obligated to obey traffic lights as the unbeliever!"—Paul J. Achtemeier, Romans, Interpretation, 204.

This chapter in Romans was important to John Calvin in formulating his doctrine of church government and his understanding of the relationship of church and state. Calvin and other reformers believed that the church should be independent of the state, but they thought that Christians should govern the state. All authority comes from God (13:1). Therefore, authority should be exercised in obedience to God, and both civil and ecclesiastical authorities should be obeyed out of respect for God.

Chapter 13 was used by German Christians as scriptural authority for obeying Adolf Hitler and thereby participating in the Nazi atrocities. Interesting, though, is the fact that those who wrote the Barmen Declaration to oppose Hitler also used this chapter as authority for declaring that Christ alone is the head of the church.

Many of the basic principles that shape the Constitution of the United States have a biblical basis through Paul's words. Civil authority is necessary in a world that has not yet experienced full redemption as children of God. Reinhold Niebuhr, using Romans as his authority, declared that the human capacity for justice makes democracy possible; the human capacity for evil makes democracy necessary.

At Romans 13:8, Paul speaks of the power of love to fulfill the law. He gives special emphasis to the Christian obligation to love one's neighbor. The neighbor is an essential member of the community and of the larger political order. The Christian life not only involves loyalty to governing officials; it calls for love of neighbor, whoever the neighbor might be.

"In Order to establish Justice . . ."

The closing verses of this chapter are a lectionary text for the First Sunday in Advent. At first reading, the verses do not seem to have special relevance to Advent. Upon closer reading, these verses speak powerfully about the attitude Christians have toward life in the present and expectations we have for the future. Advent not only celebrates the Christ who has come; it also looks forward to the return of Christ. The promised return of Christ is a constant reminder that creation will be restored by God and not by our faith or our works. For people of faith, the joy of the return of Christ is the conviction that the one who will judge creation is the one who died to redeem creation. Therefore, the judgment will be one of grace and not of condemnation (Achtemeier, 227).

The more often we hear the gospel and the more often we proclaim the

---

📖 Want to Know More?

About sacrifice? For the Old Testament context, see Werner H. Schmidt, *The Faith of the Old Testament: A History* (Philadelphia: Westminster Press, 1983), 127–32. For the New Testament context, see Bruce J. Malina, *The New Testament World: Insights from Cultural Anthropology*, rev. ed. (Louisville, Ky.: Westminster John Knox Press, 1993), 166–83.

About contemporary church and state relations? See Phillip E. Hammond, *With Liberty for All: Freedom of Religion in the United States* (Louisville, Ky.: Westminster John Knox Press, 1998) and Ronald B. Flowers, *That Godless Court? Supreme Court Decisions on Church–State Relationships* (Louisville, Ky.: Westminster John Knox Press, 1994).

About the idea of a Christian nation? See John H. Leith, *Basic Christian Doctrine* (Louisville, Ky.: Westminster John Knox Press, 1993), 199–203.

gospel, the nearer salvation comes to us. Our lives are transformed; we grow in our desire to "put on the Lord Jesus Christ" (13:14).

Attitudes toward the Weak (Romans 14)

Chapter 14 continues the theme of the Christian life as Paul writes, "Love is the fulfilling of the law" (13:8–10), but then stresses that the Christian is to go beyond the law by being concerned with the ways actions influence others.

Paul now speaks about our attitude toward the "weak." The use of the word *weak* warrants further discussion. Paul appears to see weak Christians as those who need more order or regulation in their lives. Paul's primary emphasis is that different Christians practice their faith in different ways. This has always been true and will be true, until the kingdom comes. The gospel parallels to this passage are Matthew 11:18–19; Matthew 23; and Matthew 26:6–13, which have corresponding passages in Mark and Luke. Just as people of faith in Jesus' day could not always agree as to exactly which practices honored God and which did not, so Christians in every age have disagreed about various practices. Denominational differences occur not so much because of conflict in basic beliefs as because of differences of emphasis and practice as to how to live out those beliefs. The variety of practices on issues ranging from the use of alcoholic beverages to the need for prayer books, from the form for baptism to the form for church government, illustrate the current need to be sensitive to the "weak and the strong."

This section of the letter to the Romans makes a strong plea for tolerance, not only in the specific matters addressed here but in other matters as well. Whenever one Christian tries to impose a lifestyle requirement upon another Christian, the gospel is defamed. Verses 1–12 give great freedom to the Christian in matters of behavior that are not specifically addressed in the law; verses 13–23 impose great obligation upon Christians not to use freedom in ways that alienate others.

> "[The Roman Christians] are to welcome one another because God is the great welcomer, the one whose arms are always open."—David L. Bartlett, *Romans*, Westminster Bible Companion, 123.

Again, the Pauline message is clear: To live by the grace of God is to live graciously toward others. Christians are called to accept and affirm all people without having to approve or encourage all actions.

Admonitions and Blessings (15:1–13)

Chapters 15 and 16 are not included in all the earliest manuscripts of Romans, but the message of these chapters is consistent with the previous chapters. The strong are to care for the weak. This admonition runs counter to the folk wisdom of our culture. Ben Franklin, in *Poor Richard's Almanac,* teaches that "God helps those who help themselves." Jesus and Paul teach that "God helps those who help others." The life of a Christian is a life lived in service to others, especially toward those weaker than ourselves.

In chapter 15, verses 5 and 9–12, and again in verse 13, Paul begins to conclude the letter with words of admonition and blessing addressed directly to the Romans and through them to the church universal. Achtemeier says that this portion of Romans intersects with our lives in at least three places:

1. Paul lifts our vision so that we look beyond problems we face in individual congregations and see that we are part of the larger plan of God. Our problems are not unique; solutions that worked in Paul's day will continue to work.

2. Paul helps us see the inclusive nature of God's love. In principle, no one is excluded from God's mercy.

3. Christian tolerance for those whose understanding of the life of faith requires a different response than our own is part of God's eschatological plan for harmony and peace in his creation. Recognition of the need for unity in spite of diversity is a sign of mature faith (Achtemeier, 226–27).

? Questions for Reflection

1. How can one follow the admonitions in Romans 12:14–21 and not be victimized by evil?
2. Remembering that this letter was written to a specific congregation, what ways do these chapters give guidance to the common life and interactions of the congregation today?
3. What implications does Paul's teaching about the authority of government have for Christians in situations such as the American Revolution, Nazi Germany, the Vietnam War, or the Chinese student protests in Tiananmen Square? How can one live subject to unjust authority while still opposing and resisting it?

4. Who are today's weak in faith? What are the issues of disagreement between different Christian groups? What is Paul's advice toward handling these differences? Does this seem to be a practical approach? Why?

Valedictory

Since the opening words of his letter in chapter 1, Paul has not said anything explicitly personal. Now Paul makes a transition in his style and manner of speech, reverting back to the more relational approach of the first chapter. Instead of giving instructions, he speaks closing words about himself, his plans, and specific messages to Roman Christians. Paul expresses confidence in his authority and his insights, but he realizes he may have been too bold in some of his comments (15:15). He reminds the Romans that he speaks out of personal experience of God's grace.

> "Paul saw himself, in the scheme of things, as *an instrument in the hands of Christ.* He did not talk of what he had done; but of what Christ had done with him."—William Barclay, *The Letter to the Romans*, Daily Study Bible, 203.

His broad contact with the church, and with a variety of congregations, reaffirms his authority. He asserts a particular zeal for sharing the gospel with those who have not yet heard (15:20–21).

Beginning at verse 22, Paul speaks about his travel plans. His ambitions for travel, first to Jerusalem, then to Rome, and on to Spain, would have sounded far more daring in his day than in ours.

Paul hoped to visit Rome.

The Jerusalem Offering (15:25–33)

The mention of the ministry to Jerusalem is particularly significant. Paul has been collecting an offering among the Gentile churches of Macedonia (Greece) which he writes about in great detail in 1 Corinthians 16:1–4 and 2 Corinthians 8–9. Paul appears to have a fervent hope that when the Jews in Jerusalem who have now become Christians receive this offering, the gracious Gentile generosity will create new unity and goodwill within the church. However, there is a broader way of hearing these words from Paul. Throughout the later part of Romans, Paul has grieved over the failure of many Jews to become Christians. In the spirit of Romans 12:20, the offering also may be understood as a means of bringing faith to the Jews, thereby expanding the membership of the church in Jerusalem. The Christian church had grown much faster among Gentiles than among Jews. If the Gentiles showed great concern and compassion for the Jews, in the face of the Jews' outright disregard for them, then the Gentiles' graciousness would mirror the graciousness of God, and thereby witness to the gospel. This understanding of the significance of the Jerusalem offering would reinforce the Pauline emphasis on the power of the gospel to break down dividing walls of hostility and thereby create community. For Paul, the church is not an institution or an organization; it is an embodiment of the kingdom of God, where grace reigns supreme and where all people come together as children of the one true God. To understand the Jerusalem offering in this wider context would mean that the offering becomes a practical way of living out the instructions and admonitions that begin in chapter 12.

Reconciling Those Who
Have Been Distanced

This section gives us fascinating insights into Paul's personal life and his hopes. One observer has suggested that Paul's desire to go to Jerusalem to deliver the offering in person was particularly significant and indicative of Paul's character, inasmuch as his Jerusalem enemies may have been numerous and bitter. Achtemeier says that if the Jerusalem church accepted the offering it would be an acknowledgment that Paul's apostolic mandate was valid and that his ministry would continue with the enlarged blessing of the Jerusalem Christians (Achtemeier, 230–31).

The conflict with the Jerusalem church and with the Jews had been very painful for Paul, a reminder that no matter how strong our faith, we may still have unreconciled relationships, even with people we love and respect. Paul obviously is a strong personality. Some of the admonitions in chapters 12, 14, and the opening verses of chapter 15 reflect the conflict Paul has had with other congregations, especially those in Corinth and Jerusalem. This

> "Accepting the gift is . . . tacit admission by the Jewish Christians that Jews and gentiles now stand on equal footing with respect to each other."—Paul J. Achtemeier, *Romans*, Interpretation, 230.

portion of Romans reveals Paul's pastoral nature. He longs for reconciliation with those from whom he is alienated; he is willing to take risks and undergo personal sacrifice to seek the larger good of the church.

The chapter closes with an appeal for prayer, which again indicates that Paul is nervous about the trip to Jerusalem. To understand more about Paul's relationship with the Jerusalem church, see Acts 15, which tells of a major controversy that occurred between Paul and the Jerusalem Christians. Also, chapters 21–28 tell of the controversy that occurred when Paul did reach Jerusalem. There he was ultimately arrested and sent to Rome, where he lived the remaining two years of his life.

Chapter 15 reflects a deep graciousness within Paul, even though he is tough minded. Paul and Peter are the two early Christians about whom we know the most. Both had great strengths and significant weaknesses. Both are constant reminders that it is the grace of God and the graciousness of other people toward us that give us our ultimate value. Leadership, especially in the church and in government, but also in business and civic life, always involves a certain amount of conflict, and it involves a yearning to overcome divisions that persist. We go forward by the grace of God, confident "of the fullness of the blessing of Christ," praying that "the God of peace will be with you all" (even those from whom we are estranged).

Greetings and Benediction (Romans 16)

Chapter 16 is a litany of greetings and a list of friendships Paul shared with the Roman congregations. Though in other places Paul appears to deny women roles of leadership, here he designates Phoebe as a deacon. Of all those named here, only Prisca, Aquila, Timothy, and possibly Rufus are mentioned elsewhere in the Bible. The primary value of these verses is the strong emphasis on Christian fellowship. Christian faith leads to a unique form of friendship, which transcends all sorts of boundaries.

"No doubt behind every one of these names there is a story which is a romance in Christ."—William Barclay, *The Letter to the Romans*, Daily Study Bible, 211.

The admonitions and instructions that begin in verse 17 could have been written to any congregation in Paul's time or in our own time. Once again, Paul expresses concern for those who cause dissent. Those who find joy in stirring up trouble in the church have been a source of concern from the beginning. Dealing with such individuals and groups both firmly and graciously is always a challenge.

The chapter and the book close with a benediction (16:25–27) that is an affirmation of life and a repetition of the themes in the opening salutation of the letter. Reread the greeting and benediction together carefully; note the words. The benediction places an emphasis on God, gospel, Jesus Christ, revelation, prophetic writings, Gentiles, obedience, and faith. The benediction sounds like a hymn of praise as well as words of instruction.

Romans in an Overview

Romans is about the righteousness of God and the grace of God, both of which are fully revealed and confirmed in the life, death, and resurrection of Jesus Christ. The Gospels share with us the life and faith of Jesus that led to the establishment of the church. The Acts of the Apostles tells us of the coming of the Holy Spirit, the birth of the church, and of many events in the first generation of the church's existence. Romans shares the faith of the early church in a positive proclamation. A summary of the faith proclaimed by Paul in Romans might be as follows: (1) Faith comes from God through grace. (2) Faith is inclusive, not exclusive. (3) Faith upholds the law out of respect for and obedience to God. (4) Faith leads to humility, not to arrogance or condemnation, in matters of salvation and the plan of God.

"There are no second-class people in God's eyes."—Paul J. Achtemeier, *Romans*, Interpretation, 232.

Romans also gives us insight into the early church. Paul's affirmation of the importance of Gentile congregations is significant, as is his affirmation of God's covenant of grace with the Jews. The strong message of Christian fellowship and friendship reminds us that the Christian faith is primarily relational, both horizontally and vertically. Romans is basic Christian theology, but it is far more than a book of doctrine. We get to know Paul through this book; we also get insight into Paul's knowledge of the Roman congregation and of his desire to increase that knowledge.

Romans speaks to us of the faith that formed the early church, and it shares with us the power of that faith to reform the church in every age. As the twentieth century began, scientific advances and the industrial revolution created a spirit of confidence in the future that called traditional, orthodox affirmations of Christian faith into question. Reason became more important than revelation; progress involved the elimination of mystery. Faith became captive to culture. Science and

> "The Christian's life can . . . be a time of joyful expectation, since the fulfilled promise of God is nothing less than the restoration of creation to its rightful relationship of love and devotion to its Creator and Lord."—Paul J. Achtemeier, *Romans*, Interpretation, 240.

technology held power over faith in ways similar to the ways that entertainment and recreation hold power in our time. The purpose of culture and the will of God were all too often assumed to be the same. Then came the horrors of World War I, followed by the economic collapse of the Great Depression. Science and progress could no longer guarantee a joyous future.

In 1918 the Swiss parish pastor and theologian Karl Barth wrote the first of six editions of his commentary *The Epistle to the Romans*. In the preface he wrote these words:

> Paul, as a child of his age, addressed his contemporaries. It is, however, far more important that, as Prophet and Apostle of the Kingdom of God, he veritably speaks to all [people] of every age. The difference between then and now, there and here, no doubt requires careful investigation and consideration. But the purpose of such investigation can only be to demonstrate that such differences are, in fact, purely trivial.
>
> The historical-critical method of Biblical investigation has its rightful place: it is concerned with the preparation of the intelligence—and this can never be superfluous. But, were I driven to choose between it and the venerable doctrine of inspiration, I should without hesitation adopt the latter, which has a broader, deeper, more important justification. . . .
>
> It is certain that in the past [those] who hungered and thirsted after righteousness naturally recognized that they were bound to labor with

St. Paul. . . . The reader will detect . . . that [this book] has been written with a joyful sense of discovery. The mighty voice of Paul was new to me; and if to me, no doubt to many others also (Barth, 2–3).

Barth's commentary forged the way for a genuine respect for the traditional, orthodox doctrines of Christianity combined with respect for science and technology. Revelation and inspiration are honored in this means of expressing the convictions of our faith; the Word of God is authoritative, but the capacity of the human mind to critique, reflect, and synthesize is also respected.

Want to Know More?

About the Jerusalem Collection? See Johannes Munck, *Paul and the Salvation of Mankind* (Atlanta: John Knox Press, 1959), 282–308.

About reconciliation? See R. David Kaylor, *Paul's Covenant Community: Jew and Gentile in Romans* (Atlanta: John Knox Press, 1988), 92–102.

The letter to the Romans is an affirmation of the power of the gospel to persist no matter what new information or techniques may come forth. Paul affirms the traditional teachings of faith, including the sacredness of the Old Testament and the covenant with Israel. Yet Paul also affirms the Christian faith in a carefully reasoned way, acutely aware of the challenges and questions of his day.

The Challenge of Romans for Us

For Christians living in the twenty-first century and studying Romans, the culture and historical events in that book are very different from those of the time when Augustine, Luther, Calvin, or even Barth lived. Nevertheless, Romans speaks with a power that is important for every age. The message of Romans is not out of date. Romans speaks to concerns of every generation, the nature and meaning of history, the purpose and dignity of human life, the attributes of God, and the human ability to translate our moral and spiritual obligations into acceptable actions.

As we conclude our study of Romans, we should remain ready to let Romans change the way we think and the way we perceive God, ourselves, and other people. Romans has a unique power to reform our experience of Christian faith and therefore to reform the church and all those who are members of it. We do not study Romans to "learn more about the Bible"; we study Romans to let the Word of God inform and transform our lives, that we may receive the faith of

Abraham and Sarah, the faith that is fully mature in the life, death, and resurrection of Jesus. Our faith will then bring glory to God and strengthen the church of Jesus Christ.

Barth introduced his Preface to the First Edition with these words, which provide for us a closing:

> If we rightly understand our problems, our problems are the problems of Paul; and if we be enlightened by the brightness of his answers, those answers must be ours.
>
> > Long, long ago the Truth was found,
> > A company of men it bound.
> > Grasp firmly then—that ancient truth!
>
> The understanding of history is an uninterrupted conversation between wisdom of yesterday and the wisdom of tomorrow (Barth, 1).

? Questions for Reflection

1. What have you learned about Paul the person from his letter to the Romans?
2. Review Romans 16:25–27. What is the "gospel and proclamation of Jesus Christ" to which Paul refers? How does this gospel and proclamation "strengthen you"?
3. What is the connection between trust in God and obedience to God? Which is easier for you? Why?
4. Review the definition of Christian faith that you wrote when beginning this study. How might you revise that definition now?

Bibliography

Achtemeier, Paul I. *Romans*. Interpretation. Atlanta: John Knox Press, 1985.

Bainton, Roland. *Here I Stand*. New York: Abingdon Press, 1950.

Barrett, C. K. *Reading through Romans*. London: SCM Press, 1963.

Barth, Karl. *The Epistle to the Romans*. Translated by Edwyn C. Hoskyns. London: Oxford University Press, 1933.

Bosch, David J. *Transforming Mission: Paradigm Shifts in Theology of Mission*. Maryknoll, N.Y.: Orbis Books, 1991.

Buttrick, George A. *The Interpreter's Dictionary of the Bible*. Vol. 3. New York: Abingdon Press, 1962.

Calvin, John. *Institutes of the Christian Religion*. Translated by Ford Lewis Battles, edited by John T. McNeill. Vol 1. Philadelphia: Westminster Press, 1960.

————. *Commentaries on the Epistle of Paul the Apostle to the Romans*. Translated by John Owen. Grand Rapids: Wm. B. Eerdmans Publishing Co., 1947.

Dodd, C. H. *The Epistle of Paul to the Romans*. Moffatt Commentary. New York: Harper & Brothers, 1932.

Harvey, Van A. *A Handbook of Theological Terms*. New York, Macmillan Co., 1964.

Luther, Martin. *Commentary on Romans*. Translated by J. Theodore Mueller. Grand Rapids: Kregel Publications, 1976.

Niebuhr, Reinhold. *The Nature and Destiny of Man*. Vol. 1. Louisville: Westminster John Knox Press, 1996 (1941).

————. *Beyond Tragedy*. New York: Charles Scribner's Sons, 1937.

Tillich, Paul. *Systematic Theology*. Vol. 1. (Chicago: University of Chicago Press, 1951.

Interpretation Bible Studies
Leader's Guide

Interpretation Bible Studies (IBS), for adults and older youth, are flexible, attractive, easy-to-use, and filled with solid information about the Bible. IBS helps Christians discover the guidance and power of the scriptures for living today. Perhaps you are leading a church school class, a mid-week Bible study group, or a youth group meeting, or simply using this in your own personal study. Whatever the setting may be, we hope you find this *Leader's Guide* helpful. Since every context and group is different, this *Leader's Guide* does not presume to tell you how to structure Bible study for your situation.

> "The church that no longer hears the essential message of the Scriptures soon ceases to understand what it is for and is open to be captured by the dominant religious philosophy of the moment." —James D. Smart, *The Strange Silence of the Bible in the Church: A Study in Hermeneutics* (Philadelphia: Westminster Press, 1970), 10.

Instead, the *Leader's Guide* seeks to offer choices—a number of helpful suggestions for leading a successful Bible study using IBS.

How Should I Teach IBS?

1. Explore the Format.

There is a wealth of information in IBS, perhaps more than you can use in one session. In this case, more is better. IBS has been designed to give you a well-stocked buffet of content and teachable insights. Pick and choose what suits your group's needs. Perhaps you will want to split units into two or more sessions, or combine units into a single session. Perhaps you will decide to use only a portion of a unit and then move on to the next unit. *There is not a structured theme or teaching focus to each unit that must be followed for IBS to be used.* Rather, IBS offers the flexibility to adjust to whatever suits your context.

> "The more we bring to the Bible, the more we get from the Bible." —William Barclay, *A Beginner's Guide to the New Testament* (Louisville, Ky.: Westminster John Knox Press, 1995), vii.

A recent survey of both professional and volunteer church educators revealed that their number one concern was that Bible study materials be teacher-friendly. IBS is, indeed teacher-friendly in two important ways. First, since IBS provides abundant content and a flexible design, teachers can shape the lessons creatively, responding to the needs of the group and employing a wide variety of teaching methods. Second, those who wish more specific suggestions for planning the sessions can find them at the Westminster John Knox Press web site on the Internet (**www.wjkbooks.com**). Click the "Downloads" button to access teaching suggestions for each IBS unit as well as helpful quotations, selections from Bible dictionaries and encyclopedias, and other teaching helps.

IBS is also not only teacher-friendly, it is also discussion-friendly. Given the opportunity, most adults and young people relish the chance to talk about the kind of issues raised in IBS. The secret, then, is to determine what works with your group, what will get them to talk. Several good methods for stimulating discussion are presented in this *Leader's Guide,* and once you learn your group, you can apply one of these methods and get the group discussing the Bible and its relevance in their lives.

The format of every IBS unit consists of several features:

a. Body of the Unit. This is the main content, consisting of interesting and informative commentary on the passage and scholarly insight into the biblical text and its significance for Christians today.

b. Sidebars. These are boxes that appear scattered throughout the body of the unit, with maps, photos, quotations, and intriguing ideas. Some sidebars can be identified quickly by a symbol, or icon, that helps the reader know what type of information can be found in that sidebar. There are icons for illustrations, key terms, pertinent quotes, and more.

c. Want to Know More? Each unit includes a "Want to Know More?" section that guides learners who wish to dig deeper and consult other resources. If your church library does not have the resources mentioned, you can look up the information in other standard Bible dictionaries, encyclopedias, and handbooks, or you can find much of this information at the Geneva Press Web site (see page 92).

d. Questions for Reflection. The unit ends with questions to help the learners think more deeply about the biblical passage and its pertinence for today. These questions are provided as examples only, and teachers are encouraged both to develop their own list of questions and to gather questions from the group. These discussion questions do not usually have specific "correct" answers. Again, the

> "The trick is to make the Bible our book." — Duncan S. Ferguson, *Bible Basics: Mastering the Content of the Bible* (Louisville, Ky.: Westminster John Knox Press, 1995), 3.

flexibility of IBS allows you to use these questions at the end of the group time, at the beginning, interspersed throughout, or not at all.

2. Select a Teaching Method.

Here are ten suggestions. The format of IBS allows you to choose what direction you will take as you plan to teach. Only you will know how your lesson should best be designed for your group. Some adult groups prefer the lecture method, while others prefer a high level of free ranging discussion. Many youth groups like interaction, activity, the use of music, and the chance to talk about their own experiences and feelings. Here is a list of a few possible approaches. Let your own creativity add to the list!

a. Let's Talk about What We've Learned. In this approach, all group members are requested to read the scripture passage and the IBS unit before the group meets. Ask the group members to make notes about the main issues, concerns, and questions they see in the passage. When the group meets, these notes are collected, shared, and discussed. This method depends, of course, on the group's willingness to do some "homework."

b. What Do We Want and Need to Know? This approach begins by having the whole group read the scripture passage together. Then, drawing from your study of the IBS, you, as the teacher, write on a board or flip chart two lists:

(1) Things we should know to better understand this passage" (content information related to the passage, for example, historical insights about political contexts, geographical landmarks, economic nuances, etc.] and

"Although small groups can meet for many purposes and draw upon many different resources, the one resource which has shaped the life of the Church more than any other throughout its long history has been the Bible." —Roberta Hestenes, *Using the Bible in Groups* (Philadelphia: Westminster Press, 1983), 14.

(2) Four or five "important issues we should talk about regarding this passage" [with implications for today- how the issues in the biblical context continue into today, for example, issues of idolatry or fear]. Allow the group to add to either list, if they wish, and use the lists to lead into a time of learning, reflection, and discussion. This approach is suitable for those settings where there is little or no advanced preparation by the students.

c. Hunting and Gathering. Start the unit by having the group read the scripture passage together. Then divide the group into smaller clusters (perhaps having as few as one person), each with a different assignment. Some clusters can discuss one or more of the "Questions for Reflection." Others can look up key terms or people in a Bible dictionary or track down other biblical references found in the body of the unit. After the small clusters have had time to complete their tasks, gather the entire group again and lead them through the study material, allowing each cluster to contribute what it learned.

d. From Question Mark to Exclamation Point. This approach begins with contemporary questions and then moves to the biblical content as a response to those questions. One way to do this is for you to ask the group, at the beginning of the class, a rephrased version of one or more of the "Questions for Reflection" at the end of the study unit. For example, one of the questions at the end of the unit on Exodus 3:1–4:17 in the IBS *Exodus* volume reads,

Moses raised four protests, or objections, to God's call. Contemporary people also raise objections to God's call. In what ways are these similar to Moses' protests? In what ways are they different?

This question assumes familiarity with the biblical passage about Moses, so the question would not work well before the group has explored the passage. However, try rephrasing this question as an opening exercise; for example:

Here is a thought experiment: Let's assume that God, who called people in the Bible to do daring and risky things, still calls people today to tasks of faith and courage. In the Bible, God called Moses from a burning bush and called Isaiah in a moment of ecstatic worship in the Temple. How do you think God's call is experienced by people today? Where do you see evidence of people saying "yes" to God's call? When people say "no" or raise an objection to God's call, what reasons do they give (to themselves, to God)?

Posing this or a similar question at the beginning will generate discussion and raise important issues, and then it can lead the group into an exploration of the biblical passage as a resource for thinking even more deeply about these questions.

e. Let's Go to the Library. From your church library, your pastor's library, or other sources, gather several good commentaries on the book of the Bible you are studying. Among the trustworthy commentaries are those in the Interpretation series (John Knox Press) and the Westminster Bible Companion series (Westminster John Knox Press). Divide your group into smaller clusters and give one commentary to each cluster (one or more of the clusters can be given the IBS volume instead of a full-length commentary). Ask each cluster to read the biblical passage you are studying and then to read the section of the commentary that covers that passage (if your group is large, you may want to make photocopies of the commentary material with proper permission, of course). The task of each cluster is to name the two or three most important insights they discover about the biblical passage by reading and talking together about the commentary material. When you reassemble the larger group to share these insights, your group will not only gain a variety of insights about the passage but also a sense that differing views of the same text are par for the course in biblical interpretation.

f. Working Creatively Together. Begin with a creative group task, tied to the main thrust of the study. For example, if the study is on the Ten Commandments, a parable, or a psalm, have the group rewrite the Ten Commandments, the parable, or the psalm in contemporary language. If the passage is an epistle, have the group write a letter to their own congregation. Or if the study is a narrative, have the group role-play the characters in the story or write a page describing the story from the point of view of one of the characters. After completion of the task, read and discuss the biblical passage, asking for interpretations and applications from the group and tying in IBS material as it fits the flow of the discussion.

g. Singing Our Faith. Begin the session by singing (or reading) together a hymn that alludes to the biblical passage being studied (or to the theological themes in the passage). Most hymnals have an index of scriptural allusions. For example, if you are studying the unit from the IBS volume on Psalm 121, you can sing "I to the Hills Will Lift My Eyes," "Sing Praise to God, Who Reigns Above," or another hymn based on Psalm 121. Let the group reflect on the thoughts and feelings evoked by the hymn, then move to the biblical passage, allowing the biblical text and the IBS material to underscore, clarify, refine, and deepen the discussion stimulated by the hymn. If you are ambitious, you may ask the group to write a new hymn at the end of the study! [Many hymnals have indexes in the back or companion volumes that help the user match hymns to scripture passages or topics.]

h. Fill in the Blanks. In order to help the learners focus on the content of the biblical passage, at the beginning of the session ask each member of the group to read the biblical passage and fill out a brief questionnaire about the details of the passage (provide a copy for each learner or write the questions on the board). For example, if you are studying the unit in the IBS *Matthew* volume on Matthew 22:1–14, the questionnaire could include questions such as the following:

—In this story, Jesus compares the kingdom of heaven to what?
—List the various responses of those who were invited to the king's banquet but who did not come.
—When his invitation was rejected, how did the king feel? What did the king do?
—In the second part of the story, when the king saw a man at the banquet without a wedding garment, what did the king say? What did the man say? What did the king do?
—What is the saying found at the end of this story?

Gather the group's responses to the questions perhaps encourage discussion. Then lead the group through the IBS material helping the learners to understand the meanings of these details and the significance of the passage for today. Feeling creative? Instead of a fill-in-the blanks questionnaire, create a crossword puzzle from names and words in the biblical passage.

i. Get the Picture. In this approach, stimulate group discussion by incorporating a painting, photograph, or other visual object into the lesson. You can begin by having the group examine and comment on this visual or you can introduce the visual later in the lesson—it depends on the object used. If, for example, you are studying the unit Exodus 3:1–4:17 in the IBS *Exodus* volume, you may want to view Paul Koli's very colorful painting *The Burning Bush.* Two sources for this painting are *The Bible Through Asian Eyes,* edited by Masao Takenaka and Ron O'Grady (National City, Calif.: Pace Publishing Co., 1991), and *Imaging the Word: An Arts and Lectionary Resource,* vol. 3, edited by Susan A. Blain (Cleveland: United Church Press, 1996).

j. Now Hear This. Especially if your class is large, you may want to use the lecture method. As the teacher, you prepare a presentation on the biblical passage, using as many resources as you have available plus your own experience, but following the content of the IBS unit as a guide. You can make the lecture even more lively by asking the learners at various points along the way to refer to the visuals and quotes found in the "side-bars." A place can be made for questions (like the ones at the end of the unit)— either at the close of the lecture or at strategic points along the way.

> "It is . . . important to call a Bible study group back to what the text being discussed actually says, especially when an individual has gotten off on some tangent." —Richard Robert Osmer, *Teaching for Faith: A Guide for Teachers of Adult Classes* (Louisville, Ky.: Westminster John Knox Press, 1992), 71.

3. Keep These Teaching Tips in Mind

There are no surefire guarantees for a teaching success. However, the following suggestions can increase the chances for a successful study:

a. Always Know Where the Group Is Headed. Take ample time beforehand to prepare the material. Know the main points of the study, and know the destination. Be flexible, and encourage discussion, but don't lose sight of where you are headed.

b. Ask Good Questions; Don't Be Afraid of Silence. Ideally, a discussion blossoms spontaneously from the reading of the scripture. But more often than not, a discussion must be drawn from the group members by a series of well-chosen questions. After asking each question, give the group members time to answer. Let them think, and don't be threatened by a season of silence. Don't feel that every question must have an answer, and that as leader, you must supply every answer. Facilitate discussion by getting the group members to cooperate with each other. Sometimes, the original question can be restated. Sometimes it is helpful to ask a follow-up question like "What makes this a hard question to answer?"

Ask questions that encourage explanatory answers. Try to avoid questions that can be answered simply "Yes" or "No." Rather than asking, "Do you think Moses was frightened by the burning bush?" ask, "What do you think Moses was feeling and experiencing as he stood before the burning bush?" If group members answer with just one word, ask a follow-up question like "Why do you think this is so?" Ask questions about their feelings and opinions, mixed within questions about facts or details. Repeat their responses or restate their response to reinforce their contributions to the group.

> "Studies of learning reveal that while people remember approximately 10% of what they hear, they remember up to 90% of what they say. Therefore, to increase the amount of learning that occurs, increase the amount of talking about the Bible which each member does."—Roberta Hestenes, *Using the Bible in Groups* (Philadelphia: Westminster Press, 1983), 17.

Most studies can generate discussion by asking open-ended questions. Depending on the group, several types of questions can work. Some groups will respond well to content questions that can be answered from reading the IBS comments or the biblical passage. Others will respond well to questions about feelings or thoughts. Still others will respond to questions that challenge them to new thoughts or that may not have exact answers. Be sensitive to the group's dynamic in choosing questions.

Some suggested questions are: What is the point of the passage? Who are the main characters? Where is the tension in the story? Why does it say (this)_____, and not (that) _____? What raises questions for you? What terms need defining? What are the new ideas? What doesn't make sense? What bothers or troubles you about this passage? What keeps you from living the truth of this passage?

c. Don't Settle for the Ordinary. There is nothing like a surprise. Think of special or unique ways to present the ideas of the study. Upset the applecart of the ordinary. Even though the passage may be familiar, look for ways to introduce suspense. Remember that a little mystery can capture the imagination. Change your routine.

Along with the element of surprise, humor can open up a discussion. Don't be afraid to laugh. A well-chosen joke or cartoon may present the central theme in a way that a lecture would have stymied.

Sometimes a passage is too familiar. No one speaks up because everyone feels that all that could be said has been said. Choose an unfamiliar translation from which to read, or if the passage is from a Gospel, compare the story across two or more Gospels and note differences. It is amazing what insights can be drawn from seeing something strange in what was thought to be familiar.

d. Feel Free to Supplement the IBS Resources with Other Material. Consult other commentaries or resources. Tie in current events with the lesson. Scour newspapers or magazines for stories that touch on the issues of the study. Sometimes the lyrics of a song, or a section of prose from a well-written novel will be just the right seasoning for the study.

e. And Don't Forget to Check the Web. Check out our site on the World Wide Web (www.wjkbooks.com). Click the "Downloads" button to access teaching suggestions. Several possibilities for applying the teaching methods suggested above for individual IBS units will be available. Feel free to download this material.

> "The Bible is literature, but it is much more than literature. It is the holy book of Jews and Christians, who find there a manifestation of God's presence." —Kathleen Norris, *The Psalms* (New York: Riverhead Books, 1997), xxii.

f. Stay Close to the Biblical Text. Don't forget that the goal is to learn the Bible. Return to the text again and again. Avoid making the mistake of reading the passage only at the beginning of the study, and then wandering away to comments on top of comments from that point on. Trust in the power and presence of the Holy Spirit to use the truths of the passage to work within the lives of the study participants.

What If I Am Using IBS in Personal Bible Study?

If you are using IBS in your personal Bible study, you can experiment and explore a variety of ways. You may choose to read straight through the study without giving any attention to the sidebars or other features. Or you may find yourself interested in a question or unfamiliar with a key term, and you can allow the side- bars," "Want to Know More?" and "Questions for Reflection" to lead you into deeper learning on these issues. Perhaps you will want to have a few commentaries or a Bible dictionary available to pursue what interests you. As was suggested in one of the teaching methods above, you may want to begin with the questions at the end, and then read the Bible passage followed by the IBS material. Trust the IBS resources to provide good and helpful information, and then follow your interests!

Want to Know More?

About leading Bible study groups? See Roberta Hestenes, *Using the Bible in Groups* (Philadelphia: Westminster Press, 1983).

About basic Bible content? See Duncan S. Ferguson, *Bible Basics: Mastering the Content of the Bible* (Louisville, Ky.: Westminster John Knox Press, 1995); William M. Ramsay, *The Westminster Guide to the Books of the Bible* (Louisville, Ky.: Westminster John Knox Press, 1994).

About the development of the Bible? See John Barton, *How the Bible Came to Be* (Louisville, Ky.: Westminster John Knox Press, 1997).

About the meaning of difficult terms? See Donald K. McKim, *Westminster Dictionary of Theological Terms* (Louisville, Ky.: Westminster John Knox Press, 1996); Paul J. Achtemeier, *Harper's Bible Dictionary* (San Francisco: Harper & Row, 1985).

For teaching suggestions for IBS,
click the "Downloads" button at
www.wjkbooks.com